"Every person's journey is different, whether it be the evolution so many Americans, like our president, have taken to support the freedom to marry, or the intensely personal path to accepting one's sexual orientation and building a life lived in truth in a society and amid family expectations that can make that very difficult. When Opposites No Longer Attract recounts the stories of men and women in different-sex marriages who came to terms with being gay and navigated the tugs and currents of competing concerns to be true to themselves, treat loved ones with integrity and compassion, and find happiness and wholeness."

— Evan Wolfson, Founder and President, Freedom to Marry

WHEN OPPOSITES NO LONGER ATTRACT

*Inspiring Stories of Eight
Men and Women
Who Left Straight Marriages
and Came Out as Gay*

MICHAEL TESTA

TESTA
PUBLISHING

TESTA
PUBLISHING

Published by Testa Publishing
Pittsburgh, Pennsylvania
www.testapublishing.com

ISBN: 978-0-9895917-2-0

Book and cover design by seedscreative.com
Cover photograph by Adam Milliron
Author photograph by Mike Clark

*In memory of Jane Driscoll—
I owe my life to you.*

This book is dedicated to my sons
and to the men and women throughout the world
who by coming out and expressing themselves fully
are making it possible for each of us to live freer,
more fully expressed lives.

"What is straight? A line can be straight, or a street, but the human heart, oh, no, it's curved like a road through mountains."

—Tennessee Williams, *A Streetcar Named Desire*

Contents

Author's Note

The opinions expressed in this book are my own. The people I interviewed do not necessarily agree with the opinions I express or with one another.

I have changed the names of the eight people who tell their stories in this book as well as the names of their former spouses, children, and partners. None of the people I interviewed asked for anonymity, but I wanted to protect the privacy of their families and friends. In a few cases, I also altered identifying details such as a person's profession.

My story is one of the eight included in these pages. In telling my story, I used a pseudonym for myself and for each person in my life, just as I did for all the people I interviewed. There are sections in the book—specifically in the Introduction—where I share details about my life and do not use a pseudonym. I have done that only when what I am sharing does not reveal private details about my family.

—Michael Testa
December 2013

Introduction

—Straight? Gay? Confused?—

"The cave you fear to enter holds the treasure you seek."
—Joseph Campbell

"It's a helluva start, being able to recognize what makes you happy."
—Lucille Ball

When I was growing up, there was only one model for what a romantic relationship looked like. It was simple: boy meets girl, boy marries girl, and they live happily ever after. In movies, books, fairy tales, and cartoons, that scenario was the only form for grownup love. The details would differ, but the form stayed the same. It never occurred to me that there might be another way that love and life could look.

I now know that love does not confine itself to a particular form or shape. Like water, it flows wherever there is an opening—and often goes into unexpected places. Human prejudices and dogma sometimes restrict love's flow, but nothing can keep it bound into a single artificial form forever.

In this book, I tell the story of my journey and those of seven other men and women in following the flow of love into unexpected relationships. Each of us fell in love with and married people of the opposite sex and, while married or after separating, discovered that we wanted to be with others of our own gender. Each in our own way, we found ourselves confronting some really irreconcilable differences.

Our stories recount our journeys in opening to love and the unanticipated places where love has taken us. They also tell how we each learned to be true to ourselves, even though we live in a homophobic culture in which many people consider us to be sinners, deviants, and second-class citizens.

Twenty-five years ago, I was barely conscious that the gay world existed. Today, after having been married for more than a decade to a woman and having fathered children who still live with me, I know that I am a gay man. I've come out and now identify myself as gay.

I decided to write this book because I run into a lot of men who are just like me as I used to be—married to a woman, often with children and dabbling in having sex with other men. After starting to write this book, I decided to include the stories of women as well, primarily because noticed that the lesbians I know who had been married to men handled the transition to homosexuality more gracefully and with more integrity than my male friends and I did.

The idea for this book occurred to me one night a few years ago at a bar on Pittsburgh's South Side. I was with four friends. We met there every week to watch *Will & Grace*. As we drank our beer, I realized that we were five gay men, all divorced from women we had loved, and among us, we had fourteen children. Even though I had met plenty of married men on gay sites on-line, up until that night I had considered myself an anomaly. I had lived life as a heterosexual man and didn't realize I was gay until after I was married and had children. Before that night at the bar, I had been vaguely aware that my friends and I were meeting a lot of married men—men in straight marriages—in gay bars and other venues in which these supposedly straight men were looking to hook up with other men.

That night in the South Side, it hit me that I was not an anomaly. There is something happening in American culture. People are questioning their sexual orientation. They are questioning whether they are who they thought they were. Right then, I decided to write this book. I would write the book I wish I had been able to read years ago when I was married to a woman and had young children and was starting to question whether might be gay.

—How Can You Not Know You're Gay?—

I'm sometimes asked—always by people who are straight—how it's possible not to know you're gay. To some heterosexuals, it's a straightforward question. (No pun intended.) To many gay men and lesbian women, however particularly those who are middle-aged or older, it's not an easy question to answer.

Some of the people whose stories appear in these pages tell of incidents in their lives that in hindsight suggest they probably were not straight long before they became aware of it. That was true for me.

When I was a kid, I had thoughts that I now see were about being attracted to men, but back then they were just thoughts, and I had no idea what they meant. One of my most vivid memories was of my friends' father.

I was around four or five years old, and I was enamored. He was a strong, military man. From what I recall, he stood about six feet tall and often wore his uniform and mirrored sunglasses. He stood out, and I was in awe of him. Was that my first gay moment? I have no idea, but it was something I remember clearly. I singled out a man from the crowd of people who were in my life. His three kids were my best friends. We hung out all the time. But it is their father whose memory I cherish.

Other than a few random memories like that, the whole track of my life was to meet the woman of my dreams, get married, and have kids. One of the happiest days of my life was the day I married Lynne. When I look back on the details of our wedding, I'm clear about two things: how important marriage was to me and how blind I was about being gay.

I thought the world of Lynne. She was smart and attractive and knew what she wanted in life. That was the kind of woman I had always wanted to be with. I had dreamed about my wedding day and the woman I would marry, and that woman was Lynne.

I proposed to her on my birthday. I had already spoken with Lynne's mother, who gave me her blessing to propose. Lynne's dad had passed away before I met her, or I would have spoken with him as well. The evening of my birthday, Lynne treated me to dinner, and afterward I suggested that we go to the West End Overlook, one of my favorite places in Pittsburgh.

There we stood under a streetlight, looking at the iconic view of the glowing downtown triangle formed by the Allegheny River on the left and the Monongahela River on the right, and the point where they come together to form the Ohio. It's a breathtaking sight, and like most people, we stood silently taking it in. After a few minutes, I turned toward Lynne, pulled the ring box from my coat pocket, and opened the lid. The light from the streetlamp hit the stone in the ring, fracturing into a brilliant white shimmer. I asked Lynne to marry me. She started to cry and said, "Yes."

Soon after we were engaged, we started to plan the wedding. I participated in every decision except for selecting Lynne's dress. Together she and I planned each detail—choosing the hall, meeting with too many photographers, ordering the flowers, and approving the ice sculpture we had won at a bridal show. One of the best moments was a cake-sampling party I threw at my house. I ordered sample wedding cakes from all over the area and had a party with our families to pick the one that was best.

The day of the ceremony, I instructed my ushers not to take their jackets off all night. I wanted us all to look perfect. I wanted everything to be perfect. When I walked into the church, the groomsmen were there getting ready. I inspected each of them to make sure there were no flaws. At the last second, I noticed that my cousin Bill's bottom shirt stud wasn't showing. I figured that the shirt had just pulled up a bit and that it was okay.

I found out later that the rental company had neglected to give Bill shirt studs with his tux, and the other ushers had helped him out by each giving him one of theirs. So Bill had enough shirt studs to get by although he was missing the bottom one. When I left the room, the ushers all sighed with relief that I had not caught that imperfection.

The wedding was beautiful. It was everything I had hoped it would be. The day seemed like a fairy tale. The reception hall was romantically lit and, like every detail of the ceremony and reception (except for Bill's shirt stud), it was perfect. I had planned all the details down to asking the caterer to serve the ice cream off the plate for dessert. They did it perfectly, serving scoops of vanilla ice cream in broad-bowled champagne glasses.

When I describe that detail to my gay friends today, they always laugh and say that request alone should have tipped me off to the fact that I'm gay. No straight man would have done the wedding planning I did, and it never would have occurred to a straight man to question how the ice cream would be served, let alone have a cake tasting party.

It may not sound significant that I asked the caterer to serve the ice cream off the plate. In itself, that detail is not important. But if I had been paying attention, I might have noticed that my behavior around my wedding was an example of how I don't approach life the way that most heterosexual American men do. But I wasn't paying attention to that.

I was consumed with having everything be perfect—picking the right woman, buying a flawless diamond, choosing the ideal setting to ask her to marry me, and orchestrating a fairy-tale wedding. But none of that perfection rested on a stable base. It had never occurred to me to question my sexual orientation or anything else about who I am and how I live my ife. I had no idea who I was or who Lynne was. And that eventually turned out to be a problem.

—We're Products of Our Culture—

Soon after I decided to write this book, I made an appointment to peak with a special friend of mine, Betty Hill. Betty is the Executive Director of Persad, the second oldest licensed counseling center for the lesbian, gay, bisexual, and transgender (LGBT) community in the nation. Persad was founded in Pittsburgh in 1972, at a time when homosexuality was considered a pathology in the *Diagnostic and Statistical Manual of Mental Disorders*. At that time, the common response to homosexuals was to try to treat them and help them not be who they are. That was just about forty years ago, well within this lifetime for many people.

Persad was founded on the idea of affirming the homosexual lifestyle and orientation. Instead of trying to change people or blaming issues they're having on their sexual or gender identity, Persad helps homosexual men and women deal with their issues, particularly the problems of living in a discriminatory culture. A licensed psychiatric clinic, Persad provides an array of services including mental health counseling, substance abuse treatment counseling, domestic violence services, gender transitions, and HIV/AIDS care. They also do work in HIV prevention, with youth, and with LGBT elders.

I knew that Betty could give me a useful perspective and context for this subject. She did. One of the first things she pointed out was that there is not always a clear distinction between heterosexuality and homosexuality. "I hear you distinguishing between gay men who are married to women and men who get married and then later realize they may be gay," she said to me. "You're speaking about them as though they're two different groups. I think to a degree that's true, although in some ways it's much more of a continuum."

What she went on to describe made me realize that I had been looking at sexual orientation way too simplistically. I had seen it as black and white: you were either gay or straight or possibly bisexual—although I suspected that "bisexual" was what people called themselves when they were confused about their sexual identity. I could understand how someone could be confused. I certainly had been.

Talking with Betty, I realized that what I had seen as black and white was actually a world of many shades of gray. Whereas I had viewed sexual orientation in simplistic terms, Betty's description was nuanced and complex. She spoke about the different kinds of issues that can result in a straight marriage in which one person is gay—including one's internal realities about one's orientation (such as self-awareness) and also the external and social realities that may or may not have led someone to get married or have kids.

"We do a training program in which we talk about the social context for homosexuality," Betty explained, "and I describe that context in our culture as being a triple threat. The triple threat is heterosexism, homophobia, and internalized homophobia. The effects of those three phenomena create a culture in which people do not come to know themselves easily and, whether they do or not, they're invited to conform to the majority culture and deny who they are. That's the perfect storm for both men and women to create heterosexual lifestyles for themselves even if they truly have a gay identity."

That made sense to me. I've often thought about how long it took me to become aware of myself as a gay man. I said to Betty, "When I was growing up, I didn't even know that homosexuality existed." She concurred, saying, "When I went to school, I don't think I ever heard the word *lesbian*. I never heard anyone speak it." If a word is never spoken, how can you know that the thing it names exists?

I asked Betty to tell me more about internalized homophobia. She said, "One of the unfortunate pieces of this in my opinion is that when people are trying to sort through all this, their sexuality can kind of come leaking out. The owners of bath houses and other gay meeting places will tell you that they have a lot of straight men who visit during their lunch hour or immediately following work. These are almost all married guys. That becomes one of the issues for me in terms of internalized homophobia. If you're not feeling good about yourself, you might take risks in terms of unsafe behavior that could have dire consequences. So the role of internalized homophobia—where in this process of coming to terms with your sexual identity you feel guilty and you feel awful and you're hiding and have a 'dirty secret'—that's when people do things that aren't healthy. That's troubling."

Betty explained that the heterosexual partner of a gay person experiences the same kind of heterosexism and homophobia that the gay person does. Their beliefs and religious upbringing can contribute to how dramatic their reaction is to the announcement that their spouse is gay.

she gave some examples: "I've seen married guys come out to their wives, and the wives say pretty much 'I knew it all along' and try to find a way to manage the change in their relationship in friendship. At the other end of the spectrum, there is the spouse who says, 'I'm going to kill you. You're sick. Did you give me AIDS?' It's all over the spectrum."

Issues of monogamy and betrayal can get intermingled with the issue of sexual orientation. Certainly if you're married and you've already been exploring sex outside your marriage, you have more than one issue to deal with. You have the issue of your sexual orientation and you have the issue that you're cheating on your spouse, assuming that you're in a monogamous relationship. Betty explained, "If people are coming to this discussion already married, then they're dealing with the change and the loss of an existing relationship, not just going to something new. That really makes it complicated."

Betty told me that she sees a lot of gay men who are married to women and a lot of lesbians who are married to men. "With as much heterosexism and homophobia as there are in the world, I think that most gay people experiment with trying to be heterosexual at some point," she explained. "The world doesn't just say, 'Oh, you're gay. Great. All right, next.' It's always an event in our culture. So for a kid who thinks he might be gay, his next thought is usually 'maybe not.' Being different from the norm rarely seems like a really good thing to do. You're not getting any messages that this is normal or okay, so I expect that most gay people take a whirl at being heterosexual. Some dabble in heterosexuality longer and more dramatically. Others figure it out earlier and prior to making a commitment or having kids. Regardless, I think it's common."

She told me about a study that looked at the percentage of people who identify themselves as gay and have had heterosexual sex versus those who identify as heterosexual who've had homosexual experiences. The difference was dramatic: about 87 percent of the gay people in the study had had heterosexual experiences whereas about 23 percent of the straight participants had had homosexual experiences.

"That's a huge disparity," she said. "People talk a lot about kids experimenting with their sexuality. If it were just a matter of people experimenting, the percentages would be about the same. The fact that it's four times more likely for a gay person to have straight sex than for a straight person to have gay sex suggests that there is a bias toward heterosexuality.

"We're all invited to be straight. We're all invited to get married to someone of the opposite sex and have kids. So why should we be shocked that there are a lot of gay people who are or have been in straight marriages and have kids? Marriage and kids are what your parents were planning for you since you were born. It's what you were taught in school. It's what there is to do."

—How Common Is It for People to Leave a Straight Marriage and Come Out as Gay?—

As you might guess, it is difficult to get statistics on how many people leave straight marriages and come out as gay. I've come to think that there aren't even reliable estimates about how many gay people there are. One problem in estimating the number of homosexuals is that there is no standard definition of what homosexuality is. Are we talking about people who have some sexual contact with a same-sex partner, more same-sex than opposite-sex contact, or exclusive same-sex contact?

Alfred Kinsey, who conducted authoritative research on sexual behavior in the United States in the 1940s and 1950s, concluded that it is not possible to determine how many people are homosexual and how many are heterosexual. All one can do is identify individual behavior at a particular time.[1]

To conduct his research, Kinsey had highly trained assistants conduct in-depth interviews with 5,300 men and 5,940 women. The subjects were mostly younger white adults with some college education. Kinsey found that among the men, 37 percent had at least one sexual experience with another man that resulted in orgasm, 10 percent were predominantly homosexual as adults, 8 percent were homosexual exclusively for three years or more, and 4 percent had been homosexual exclusively from adolescence on. Among the women, 13 percent had at least one same-sex sexual encounter, 2 to 6 percent were "more or less exclusively homosexual," and 1 to 3 percent were "exclusively homosexual in experience/response."[2]

Kinsey and his colleagues developed a seven-point scale for classifying individual sexual behavior, with Heterosexual at one end and Homosexual at the other and varying gradations of same-sex and opposite-sex experience and response between these two extremes. A drawing of the Kinsey Scale is shown. Commenting on the scale in their book *Sexual*

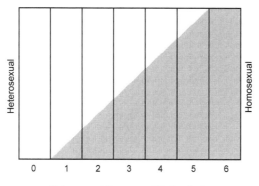

Heterosexual-Homosexual Rating Scale

- Exclusively heterosexual
- Predominantly heterosexual, only incidentally homosexual
- Predominantly heterosexual, but more than incidentally homosexual
- Equally heterosexual and homosexual
- Predominantly homosexual, but more than incidentally heterosexual
- Predominantly homosexual, only incidentally heterosexual
- Exclusively homosexual

Behavior in the Human Male, Kinsey and his coauthors wrote, "Males do not represent two discrete populations, heterosexual and homosexual. The world is not divided into sheep and goats. Not all things are black nor all things white.... Only the human mind invents categories and tries to force facts into separated pigeon-holes. The living world is a continuum in each and every one of its aspects. The sooner we learn this concerning human sexual behavior the sooner we shall reach a sound understanding of the realities of sex."[3]

When the first Kinsey report was published in 1948, it was met with both criticism and praise. It was a groundbreaking work, as was the report on female sexual behavior, which was published five years later.

Some people think that Kinsey's findings can be interpreted as evidence of bisexuality. I think it is just as logical to interpret them as evidence of waffling. In a homophobic culture, it takes insight and courage—and for some people, time—to recognize oneself as homosexual, and it can be painfully difficult to choose a life that is radically different from the way most people live.

If I look at my own history, I can say that I now lean more toward being exclusively homosexual on the Kinsey Scale, although I am not repulsed by women as some gay men are. It took me a long time to discover that and to tell the truth about it. Twenty-five years ago, I would have been just as adamant that I was straight. There's a saying in the gay community: There are no bisexuals, only gays and lesbians and people on the fence.

A 1994 survey by *The Advocate* seems to offer support for that view. The survey found that 40 percent of gay men had previously identified themselves as bisexual.[4]

Further evidence is provided by a study reported in 2005 in *Psychological Science.*[5] Psychologists in Chicago and Toronto recruited 101 men—30 heterosexuals, 33 bisexuals, and 38 homosexuals. Alone in a room, each man was shown erotic movies, some depicting men and others depicting women. Genital arousal was measured, and each man indicated his own arousal.

The men who identified themselves as bisexual did not show strong sexual arousal to both men and women. Instead, about three-quarters of them responded strongly to images of males, and the rest responded strongly to images of females. Compared to heterosexual and homosexual men, the bisexual men also showed a greater discrepancy between their subjective measure of arousal and the objective measure.

To be fair, the study has its critics. According to an article in *The New York Times*, one primary criticism was that "the technique used in the study to measure genital arousal is too crude to capture the richness—erotic sensations, affection, admiration—that constitutes sexual attraction."[6] I don't know whether the criticism is warranted or not. What I can say is that the study appears to provide pretty strong evidence that, at least for some people, bisexuality is a state of transition or confusion.

Drew, one of the men who shared his story in this book, would probably agree with that. During our interview, he said, "It's not unusual for married men to ask me out. I tell them that I won't go out with a married man. 'Go divorce your wife and then I'll go out with you.' Drew said that in response, they all say that same thing: 'But I'm not gay! I'm bi.' They're not bisexual. That's just an excuse. They're just trying to straddle the fence."

Let's get back to the question of how many Americans are gay. A recent study by The Williams Institute of the UCLA School of Law found that nearly nine million adults in the United States identify themselves as gay, lesbian, bisexual, or transgender. That is almost 4 percent of American adults. The study also found that 19 million adults have had sex with someone of the same gender, and more than 25 million people—11 percent f Americans—acknowledge being attracted to others of the same sex.[7]

When it comes to how many people in straight marriages may not ctually be straight, the numbers are fluid to say the least, but they do suggest hat this is not a rare phenomenon.

In a 2006 article in *The New York Times*, Jane Gross reported that, n the 1970s and '80s, studies found that between 20 and 33 percent of gay nen were or had been in straight marriages. The article also reported on he findings of Gary J. Gates, a demographer at The Williams Institute of he UCLA law school. Analyzing data from the 2000 Census and a 2002 ʲderal survey of families, Gates found that the percentage of gay men who ad been in straight marriages could range from 9 percent to 38 percent epending on the questions the men were asked.[8]

He found that 1.6 percent of the 27 million American men who were ʲarried at the time of the survey identified themselves as gay or bisexual. That ʲercentage doubled when the men were asked if they had ever had sex with ther men. The percentages were similar among the 75 million American ʲen who had ever been married: 1.8 percent identified themselves as gay or ʲisexual, and twice that number responded that they had had male sexual ʲartners.[9]

A survey conducted in 2003 of more than four thousand men in New ʲork City found that a significant number of men who have sex with other ʲen consider themselves to be straight. Reported in the *Annals of Internal ⱽedicine*, the survey found that nearly 10 percent of the men who identified ʲemselves as straight had sex with one or more men in the preceding year, ʲnd almost 70 percent of those men were married to women.[10] What was ʲost surprising to me was that, of the men who engaged in sex with other ʲen, almost 73 percent called themselves heterosexual.[11]

I asked each of the men and women I interviewed how common they ʲink it is for people in a straight marriage to come out as gay or lesbian. Do ʲey personally know people who are or were in a straight marriage who ʲave come out or are having homosexual encounters? I wanted to find out ʲ they thought that the eight of us are examples of a much more widespread ʲhenomenon.

All agreed that we are not an anomaly. All eight of us know people ʲho have left straight marriages and come out as gay. But there was a distinct ʲifference in the responses by gender when I asked if they know people in ʲ straight marriage who are having homosexual sex. All the men (including me) know a lot of men who are married to women and having sex with other men. None of the women knew anyone—male or female—who fit that description.

Trudy's response was typical of the answers the women gave. She said, "I have several friends who are lesbian and were married to men. They're my age. We have a lot in common. I hang with a group of people who all left heterosexual marriages. I don't know people who are married and haven't come out yet because my world is very gay."

Kathy, who considered herself heterosexual until her late thirties, said, "When I was coming out and I started telling some of my straight friends who were married, some of them told me that they'd felt attracted to women too. It was interesting. I don't think any of them had acted on it. A few had maybe experimented in the past but not while they were married to a man. So I did experience that—women who are married to men and had been with women in the past or felt attraction to women. I was surprised at how many women told me that."

Adam said that there are a lot of men in straight marriages who are having sex with other men, but he wouldn't necessarily call them "gay." Here's how he explained it: "I think that people are becoming freer about having sex with someone of the same gender, and I think there are a lot of married men who are having sex with other men, but that doesn't make them gay. To me, homosexuality and being gay are different. Homosexuality is purely about physical attraction, the physical part of sex, whereas gay is a culture. Gay means wanting to be in a relationship with another man. It's more woven into the fabric of who you are; it's not just an aspect of who you are. It's how you identify yourself."

I'm meeting more and more men who are married to women and having sex with other men. Some consider themselves straight and think they're walking on the wild side. Other men are clearly in the closet, aware they're attracted to men but unwilling to come out for fear of hurting their family or losing their job or simply because they don't know what to do. Still others are simply unaware.

I was once like that. It wasn't until I was in my mid-thirties that I started to suspect that I am not straight. Sometimes I still question whether I'm gay or straight.

I'm writing this book to shed light on this phenomenon. There are lots of people struggling with issues of their sexual identity and their on't know what to do. Some of those people are married, and that makes confronting the truth—whatever it is—possibly even messier.

I want to be clear that I am not advocating cheating and I am not advocating divorce. Quite the opposite—I'm committed to marriage. In fact, I'm fighting for it in the gay community. I'm on the board of Equality Pennsylvania and I'm a member of Freedom to Marry. My intention is not to break up families. But is a family really together when one spouse is cheating on the other? Is a family together when one spouse is living a secret life?

My intention is not to recruit anyone to the gay life. What I hope to do is shine light on the subject of people questioning their sexual identity while married to someone of the opposite sex. Very little has been written about this. I believe it can be supportive to know that you're not alone—that others are dealing with the same kinds of issues that you are. I believe we can learn from one another—that knowing how someone handled a difficult situation successfully can help you handle your challenge successfully as well.

—The People Who Share Their Stories in This Book—

The information for this book came from interviews with eight men and women who left straight marriages for homosexual relationships. I chose to interview them because I know them. I am not a social scientist. I do not have research skills. My intention is to allow people who have made the transition from the straight world to the gay world to share their experience in the hope that it might prove useful to others.

The people I interviewed are perfect for the task, primarily because we (I include my own story) are all so normal. We all live in and around Pittsburgh, Pennsylvania. Pittsburgh is a small city—sixty-first of the one hundred largest U.S. cities by population in 2012. (We were the eighth largest in 1910. Pittsburgh is not actually shrinking, simply not expanding its boundaries to annex its suburbs the way Sun Belt cities do.)

Located on the western edge of the East Coast and the eastern edge of the Midwest, Pittsburgh is a friendly city that seems to have escaped big-city pretensions and middle-American stodginess. The city has adapted well to the loss of its steel industry to become a leader in health care, robotics, and technology. No one would confuse Pittsburgh with Chelsea in New York or the Castro District of San Francisco, but in 2011 *The Advocate* ranked us fifth in its list of the fifteen gayest cities in America. (In 2012, Pittsburgh dropped to number nineteen on the list. In 2013, we didn't make it onto the list at all.)

I'm mentioning these details to underscore my point that the people who share their stories in this book are average Americans. We are not that different from people living anywhere in the U.S. If this phenomenon is happening in Pittsburgh, it is happening across this country. There are people everywhere in straight marriages who are questioning whether they are in fact straight.

Now I'd like to introduce you to the people whose stories appear in these pages. As I mentioned in the note at the beginning of this book, the people I interviewed did not ask me to change their names, but I decided to do that to protect the privacy of our former spouses, our partners, and our children.

The eight people who tell their stories here share personal details about how they came to marry and also how they came to realize that they are not straight. All our stories are different.

❖ For as long as he can remember, **Adam** has been attracted to both men and women. He fell in love with Kate and married her, and he is still in love with her, even though he now lives as a gay man.

❖ **Kathy** began questioning her sexual orientation when she was in her thirties and engaged to Nick. She talked with him about what was happening. Nick insisted that she get help. Three months after they married, she left him.

❖ It had never occurred to **Drew** that he was anything but straight until he found himself attracted to men as his relationship with Susan became unbearable. Not long after they married, Susan became physically abusive, and the violence escalated over their eleven years together. Drew found solace initially in the friendships he formed with men and then in sexual relationships with men.

❖ **Trudy** knew from a young age that she was attracted to girls and uncomfortable around boys, but an incident in high school convinced her that she should marry a man and have children. She believes that decision probably saved her life.

❖ **Gene** always knew he was gay, but he married Casey because he loved her and didn't want to be gay anymore. Their marriage lasted for twelve years. Toward the end, they were living like brother and sister.

❖ Like Kathy and Drew, **Erin** never questioned being anything but heterosexual until she was in her thirties. At the time, she was separated from her husband of eleven years. Ten years after she came out, she met the love of her life.

❖ Prior to marrying Marin, **Ben** had only one sexual encounter with a man. At the time, he believed that being with men was not an option for him, however, so he shelved that part of himself. A few years later when he began traveling for work, he started having sex with men. He and Marin eventually separated.

❖ **Grace** had always considered herself to be straight until she realized that she was deeply attracted to Christine. At the time, she was married to Luke. She was completely open with him about her feelings for Christine. Luke ultimately gave her his support in ending their marriage so Grace could be with Christine.

I find all these stories worth telling. Coming out as gay was not easy for any of us. Each of us had a heterosexual life and a spouse, and most of us had one or more children. Each had to come to terms with the fact that he or she was not heterosexual. Coming out is the public declaration of that fact. It can be a terrifying conversation to anticipate having. As these stories show, there is no right way to come out.

I asked each person the same questions, but I allowed them to tell their own stories in their own way. As a result, some stories are long, with a lot of detail, while others are shorter. One question I asked each person was if they had any advice for others who are in the position they were once in. The most common advice had to do with the question, What should you do if you're in a heterosexual marriage and experiencing homosexual attractions? Several people spoke about how important it is to talk with your spouse. Others gave advice about coming out, what to do if you have kids, and the importance of getting support.

Not everyone offered advice, but most did. I've included a section of advice at the end of each person's story. All the people I interviewed left straight marriages for same-sex relationships. Having gone through that we're all in a good position to offer our experience and some of the wisdom we've gained. Not all of the advice is consistent. Different people offer different perspectives. What became apparent to me as I spoke with each person is that there is no one way—and no right way—to deal with what to do if you're in a straight marriage but questioning if you are indeed straight.

I look at this book as a guide for how to be true to oneself. It provides a glimpse into a world that most people are not aware of, in which men and women are coming to terms with who they are and getting to know an aspect of themselves, often for the first time. Self-knowledge is a good thing. However, when your new awareness has to do with your sexual orientation and your newfound orientation is not compatible with that of your spouse, it's clear you've got a problem. How can you be true to yourself without causing pain to yourself and others?

I believe that there is power in telling the truth. The truth shall set you free. This is a subject that's been cloaked in darkness and shame for too long. It's time for us to shine light on it. The truth can set us all free.

Part 1

In Our Own Words:

The Stories of the People Interviewed

Chapter 1

Adam

Even as a kid, Adam was attracted to both males and females. "I would watch *The Brady Bunch*, and I was attracted to one of the boys," he said. "But from time to time I was also attracted to Marsha." As a young man, Adam was intimate with both men and women—more women, he explained, because he was nervous about getting AIDS. He married Kate in 1987 after they dated for eighteen months. He was in love with Kate then and is still in love with her today. They separated after more than twenty years together after she hugged him tenderly one day and said, "Now it's time for you to be you." They have three adult children. Adam is now fifty-one and runs a marketing company. Since he gave this interview, he has begun a serious relationship with a man.

—Adam's Story—

When did I realize I was gay? You know, I always knew, since I can remember, even when I was really little, having an attraction to men. I've known all my life that I was different. I would watch television and I was attracted to one of The Monkees, or as I got older I was attracted to one of the Bradys—and it wasn't usually Marsha. It's not like I swept it under the carpet, but rather I kind of disregarded it. Now, to be honest, I also from time to time was attracted to Marsha.

So, I guess I was confused. I wasn't sure who I was attracted to. I was attracted to a lot of people. It wasn't until I was in high school that I started to tune in to having feelings for guys. Even so, I dated girls in high school. I've always dated females. Then in college, I kind of went on retreat from being attracted to guys and began an on-again, off-again love affair with my gayness.

That was way before I met and married Kate.

—Marriage—

Kate and I met in graduate school. We were graduate assistants at the same university. I was very attracted to her. I remember meeting her one time at a bar with a bunch of people and feeling very attracted to her but not acting on it. Then, she and I both started working at the same place, and I'd see her every day. A co-worker told me that she was married. He made that assumption because she had a child. But I wanted to know for sure, so I walked up to her and asked, "Are you married?" She said no, and I finally asked her out.

About two weeks after we started dating, I told Kate that I was gay—that I was attracted at least sometimes to men. I told her right away. Because she had a child, I needed to step up to a higher level of responsibility. Maybe that's because I didn't have that when I was growing up. I had my mom, but I didn't really know my father. He left when I was very young. I spent time with him—a week now and then, and once I stayed with him for a year. But it was like spending time with a stranger—even when I spent a year with him. I didn't know him, and I didn't want to be like him.

I made a decision early in my life that whenever I got married, I wanted to have children and be a good father. All those things were going through my mind when I met Kate. It wasn't like someday we might have kids, and then I'd have to consider them. It was instant, because she already had a child.

When you fall in love with someone who has a child, you have to be cognizant of that. If my being attracted to men was going to be a deal breaker for Kate, I didn't want to tell her a year or two into the relationship. I didn't want to take a child down that path. Her child had already lost one father, and I didn't want to get involved with them and then reveal something to Kate that might have her stop seeing me.

So two weeks into our relationship, I felt that I had to come clean with Kate. I told her that I'd had sex with both men and women. I'd been with more women than men. In my teens and early twenties, there was a lot about AIDS in the news. It was a new thing. To be honest, my fear of AIDS probably caused me to go a little deeper into the closet. It was scary and intimidating to me, and frankly I realized that my feelings for men weren't that strong. It wasn't worth it. Plus, I'd always wanted a family. That was a big thing for me.

My coming out to her was not a deal breaker for Kate. She took it well, and we stayed together. At the time, it helped that we both worked in a field that's filled with liberal-minded people.

We dated for about eighteen months before we got married. I legally adopted Kate's daughter, and we had three other children, one of whom died a few days after birth.

I was in love with Kate then, and I'm still head over heels in love with her.

We were a famously perfect couple. I think everybody was shocked when we separated. We had a storybook marriage, and to be honest it wasn't just for appearances. It was real. There was very little contention between us. We had good financial stability, four amazing children, and a great family life. We had fun together. We traveled together. We looked forward to spending time together. It was all very good. We lived together for over twenty years.

So why aren't we together now? That's what everybody wants to know. I can't even remember what specifically started it, but it came out of my having a massive panic attack. I started having feelings for men resurface. I always used to sweep it under the carpet when I'd start to have feelings for men come up. I'd say to myself, *Right now, your time needs to be focused on raising your family and on being a good father and husband. Your time will come when the kids are older.*

I'd made a commitment that I would never walk away from raising my kids. What caused my anxiety was that I realized that I'd been saying for years that my time would come. Well, my time had come. My time was now. Our kids were grown, and I started freaking out.

I think in my wife's case, there was part of her that felt it was unfair to her to be married to a gay man. For the first twenty years of our married life, we had a very fulfilling sex life. Then everything started to derail for me. It wasn't that I didn't feel attracted to my wife—who, I have to say, is gorgeous. She's a ten. People used to say to me, "She's married to you?"

So it wasn't that I wasn't attracted to her. It was probably more that I felt guilty about what I was thinking and feeling and wanting to do. It was never her fault. There was never anything she didn't give me. She provided for me emotionally and physically. She never left a void in my life. Despite all that, our sex life fizzled.

I think Kate needed to free herself and she needed to free me at the same time. She said to me finally that she had wondered when this was going to happen. She said she felt a sense of relief now that it was happening, and she didn't have to wonder about it anymore.

—Separation—

When we separated, it wasn't like we had big fights. I remember that we were standing in the kitchen, and she just really tenderly hugged me and said, "All your life, you've been whoever people wanted you to be. Now it's time for you to be you. I love you, and I want you to be happy. You know we'll always be the best of friends, and we'll always be parents together." She was so sweet and loving.

At the time, I thought she was right. Now I think that love trumps desire. When I came out of the closet, men would say, "Oh, man, you need to go out and have fun." The stereotype is that when it comes to sex, men are like diners in a sushi restaurant—they want to have a whole boatload. That's not me. I'm a lover. If I'm deeply in love with someone, I'm not somebody who can just go out and randomly have sex. That's just not my M.O.

Since our separation, it's been a difficult three years for me, because Kate is perfect for me and I'm still deeply in love with her. I've asked her several times to take me back, and she won't. She says that I'm not allowing myself to be who I am and I need to free myself. I don't know if this is what you want to put in the book or not, but that's my experience.

She and I still get along really well. We're like two really good friends, and we're still a team when it comes to parenting our kids. I always say, if you really love someone, when the relationship ends, you can't just turn your love off. You just have to kind of switch it over to a different kind of love. I'm still happiest when I'm with either Kate or one of our kids. My family is my mainstay.

I'm a little nervous right now. In two weeks, I'm going to the beach with Kate and our kids. To be honest, I am nervous about it. I'm not nervous because I'm afraid there'll be problems. I'm nervous because I'm wondering if it's the healthiest thing for me to put myself into this situation when I have such strong feelings for her still.

—Coming Out—

Telling my children that Kate and I had decided to separate was one of the hardest things I've ever had to do. I still have flashbacks of their sadness.

Kate and I told our kids—who were all in their late teens and twenties at the time—that we were separating, and honestly you would've thought that we had told them that everybody they loved had just died. They completely lost it. They cried. They all held each other. My son, who was a junior in high school at the time, said, "Please tell me this is a nightmare." My kids were a mess.

I'll tell you what was sad about it. They were all so excited when we called them into the living room to talk. Every other time we've done that, it was to tell them that we were going on a cruise or taking a trip to Disney World. They were anticipating something happy and magical, and instead we told them we were splitting up. They were devastated.

Coming out to them was part of the same conversation. I didn't expect it to go well given how they'd reacted to the news of the separation. I was shocked by their response.

After they got a little composure, we told them why we were getting separated, and things settled down. I let everybody know that I was going down to the family room. I suggested that they all spend some time with their mom, and if anybody wanted to talk to me, they could join me one at a time.

The first person to come down to see me was my son-in-law. He's married to my oldest daughter, and he's a part-time pastor. He hugged me and said, "In my twenty-nine years of life, I've never learned more about being a man than I've learned tonight." And this is a man who still wears the ring he earned from being in a college football championship. He's a man's man.

Then his wife, my oldest daughter, came in. She said, "I love you, and I always will. This doesn't change anything."

Then my middle daughter came down and hugged me and whispered in my ear that I was her hero. She said, "So many people live their lives never being who they're meant to be." Then, of course, she asked if this meant that I would now take her shopping for clothes. I told her it didn't. I didn't get that gene.

And then my son came down and told me he loved me. I was crying, and he said, "Dad, it's okay. It's no big deal. You're just gay. Lots of people are gay."

I was just as surprised by how the rest of our family reacted.

Kate and I were terrified to tell her parents, who are wonderful people, but they're very traditional and conservative. But we had to tell them. So we made the trip to their home and spoke with them. After we did, my father-in-law grabbed my hand and said, "As far as I'm concerned, you're still the same great man that I handed my daughter over to twenty-three years ago." And my mother-in-law said, "Well, since you can't be my son-in-law now, I guess you're gonna have to be my son."

I'm still invited to every family function. They all call me. They send me cards. They come over for my birthday. My mother-in-law calls me regularly to see how I'm doing, just like she calls all her kids.

I've been fortunate, to say the least.

—Adam's Life Now—

Legally, Kate and I are still married. That's more for practical reasons—such as health care and our kids, to be honest.

Since she and I separated, I've been dating men. For a while, there was a woman I found myself attracted to. We talked a few times, and we were flirtatious. And I'd think, *Oh, okay, how much more complicated can I get here?*

I'm a romantic, and I'm traditional. Everything about me is the traditional romantic man with the exception that I also like to have sex with men. I don't know if that makes sense.

One thing you could say about me is that when I love, I love deeply. If I ever say I'm in love, then you know I'm really in love, because I don't throw that term around often or lightly.

This is a really tough thing for me to say. Sex with a man is one thing, but I have a hard time getting lovey-dovey with a man. It doesn't click for me. I feel like the deepest—the most romantic—I could get with a man is when I'm having sex with my best buddy. Being romantic just feels too uncomfortable for me. I always tell women that I don't know how they deal with men. Men are absolute assholes—every single one of them. They all think with their crotches.

I'm happy, and I've got a good life, despite the fact that I miss Kate a lot. At the same time, I've enjoyed getting to know me. For the first time, without fear or anxiety, I'm getting to know what's important to me. So I'm doing well.

I never really knew what it was like to spend time by myself. My whole life has been about taking care of others and being with others, so this is really the first time in my life that I've spent alone. What's funny is that I'm not lonely. In fact, I kind of like it. I've become very independent and I like that, which is something of a barrier to dating. I think I'm a little selfish right now. I don't want to have my life revolve around someone else.

Just the other day, I was planning a vacation for myself, and I was having so much fun. It was fun to consider just one thing: What do I want to do? That felt really good and healthy to me. I don't have to compromise right now with anybody.

—Advice—

Children

If you're a parent, in my opinion, that responsibility never changes throughout life. However you choose to live your life, and whatever happens between you and your spouse, don't make it the responsibility of your children. The only real act of selfishness is to deny your children good parenting and to pull them into your drama. Always love your kids and always be the best partners you can possibly be as parents. That's the aspect of a partnership that should never end. Kids deserve a team.

What Should You Do?

Here's my advice to a man who's married to a woman and attracted to men: Enjoy your attraction to men without acting on it. If you're in love with your wife, don't feel that you've got to step away from that. Enjoy your attraction. Enjoy another man's beauty, but recognize that there are limitations and boundaries.

Commitment is commitment. You have to say, "I'm married and I'm committed so I'm not going to get emotionally involved and I'm not going to step outside my marriage by having sex with someone else—whether it's a man or a woman." But don't feel bad that you find men attractive. Enjoy it.

On the other hand, if you really are gay and married to a woman, free yourself and free her. But do it in a loving way. Try to preserve what brought the two of you together in the first place. Preserve what you can. It's worth it in the end.

Other than that, the most important advice I have is to be yourself. You've got to do it how you want to do it. There's no road map. There's no particular way your life has to look. Lots of people will tell you that you have to do things a certain way. Personally, I don't want to have to do things a certain way. Just because I'm gay, I don't want to feel like I have to vacation in P-town or Rehoboth or Key West, and I don't want to have to march down Liberty Avenue on Gay Pride Day. I didn't do "have to" kinds of things as a heterosexual, and I don't do them now.

I recommend you get to know yourself and love yourself. Love the process.

Chapter 2

Kathy

Kathy was the first woman I interviewed for this book. Talking with her made me question whether women approach the transition from straight life to homosexuality differently than men do. Kathy was thirty-eight and engaged to Nick when she first questioned seriously whether she might be gay. She talked about it with him. Nick believed that being gay is a choice and insisted that Kathy get help. At his urging, she went to three different psychiatrists, each of whom said there was nothing wrong with her. Kathy married Nick in August 2002 and left him three months later. She lives in Pittsburgh and works as a business coach. Kathy is in a long-term relationship with Sarah.

—Kathy's Story—

I was a tomboy growing up. Looking back, I can see that as a girl I was attracted to women. I had a huge crush on Angie Dickinson. But I never would go there. I never dealt with my sexuality. In college, I played on the golf team and even then pretty much everybody was in the closet. I didn't know anyone who was openly gay. Homosexuality was still very much a taboo subject. I didn't find college to be a safe place.

I was attracted to a woman on the golf team, and I think she was attracted to me, but we never acted on it, we never talked about it, we never went there. I never even admitted to myself that I could be a lesbian. I justified that I wasn't gay by saying, "I'm not attracted to lesbians." Rosie O'Donnell was a well-known lesbian, and my rule of thumb was that, if I'm not attracted to her, then I must not be a lesbian.

I never dealt with my attraction to women until I was thirty-eight years old. That's when I first questioned my sexuality—that I might be gay. But I still couldn't even say the word.

What happened was that I found myself attracted to a woman who was leading a course I was in, and I found out afterward that she was gay. That blew my whole rationalization that I was not gay. I'd never been attracted to a gay woman, and all of a sudden—oh, my God—I was attracted to a gay woman. My world stopped. Everything shattered.

It was a Landmark Education program. She and I have since become very good friends. She was the first person I came out to.

At the time, I was engaged to be married to Nick, a man that I'd been with for almost nine years. He and I were finally ready to get married, so my coming out was life altering—actually life shattering. It was very destructive to my life as I knew it to realize that I was attracted to a lesbian.

—Coming Out—

Nick and I were planning to go to New York and have a small wedding. My brother and his wife were going to be there, plus my best friend and her husband. I came out to my friend. She said, "You have to tell Nick." I remember going with him to a pizza place for dinner, and I told him that I was questioning my sexuality. It was exactly four weeks before we were scheduled to be married.

Nick was shocked. His mouth dropped open. He didn't say anything for the longest time. I knew that he thought that being gay was a choice that one makes. Finally he said, "I'll pay for whatever psychologist, psychiatrist, or doctor you need. You have two weeks to get fixed."

Two weeks? To "get fixed"?

And this was someone I loved. We'd created a life together. It was very upsetting. I could not imagine not spending the rest of my life with Nick, but I also couldn't imagine spending the rest of my life not knowing who I am. So I told him that I'd talk to a therapist, and I started making appointments.

I saw three different therapists in the next two weeks. Each one told me the same thing: there was nothing wrong with me. One explained to me the Kinsey theory that some people are straight, some are gay, and most are somewhere in the middle. When you're in the middle, he said, it can be kind of confusing.

He gave me a test to see where I was along the Kinsey continuum. Was I straight, or gay, or in the middle? I lied about some of my answers. It was an oral test, and the therapist asked questions like, In this situation, do you find yourself more attracted to women or to men? Whenever I was in doubt, I would choose men. I think I was hoping that somehow I'd be able to come out of this still marrying Nick and putting my attraction to women behind me. For thirty-eight years I never dealt with it, and I was hoping to shut that door again and not have to deal with it anymore.

I came home to Nick—I was living with him at the time—and I said, "Good news—I'm bisexual." Given that the test showed me to be bisexual, I took that to mean that I could marry Nick. Being bisexual meant that I could be with both men and women. I was already engaged to Nick, so I decided to go ahead and marry him.

—Marriage—

A few weeks later, Nick and I were married. We stayed together less than three months. We got married on August 31, and I left in November. I think it was on my birthday.

What I discovered after we got married was that once I'd told the truth to myself about my sexuality, it didn't go away. I couldn't see spending the rest of my life not fulfilling on something like that—and I wasn't willing to cheat on Nick. I had a sense of authenticity about my sexuality. I had a sense that that's who I am—but I had no validation for it at all. At that point, I'd never had sex with a woman. I'd never even kissed a woman.

So about three months into our marriage, I said to Nick, "This is not going away. I'm still questioning whether I'm gay." Nick did not handle it well. One day I came home, and he had packed up all my stuff. So I left.

At that moment, it was more his choice than mine that I should leave. Before that, he'd kept trying to fix the situation. He wanted me to quit my job, to get help, to do whatever it would take to have everything be back to normal. He wanted to take care of me.

My mom had died when I was eleven, and I've always had a sense that my mom's been with me saying, *You just gotta be happy. Go for happy.* And it doesn't matter what it looks like to be happy. I just felt that I couldn't spend the rest of my life not knowing whether I was gay or straight. I left my marriage without even knowing which I was.

Looking back now, I think Nick and I probably would have grown apart anyway if I hadn't left when I did. It was a big risk for me to leave, but I felt like I had to take it. I had to find out who I am. I had that sense that, when you tell the truth, you may not like it, but you know it's true for you. There's a saying I've heard: The truth will set you free, but first it'll piss you off. There were times when I didn't want it to be true that I'm gay, but I knew it was true, and I had to deal with that.

I did love Nick. We had our whole life planned out—what we were going to do, when we were going to retire. Everyone who knew us thought we probably had the best relationship on the planet. After we broke up, I started telling some of our friends why I'd left. Initially, Nick wanted me to do that because he thought they would tell me I was crazy—that there was something wrong with me. But when it turned out that my friends were accepting—like the therapists had been—he didn't want me to tell anyone else. So at that point I left Indianapolis, where we lived, and I moved to Cincinnati, because I just couldn't deal with not being able to share that part of me. People kept asking why we had broken up, and I didn't want to have to choose between telling the truth and having him be even more upset than he already was.

Nick wouldn't forgive me, and he really never believed it was true that I was gay. He told people that I went crazy. I talked to him once after I moved to Pittsburgh in 2005. It was a cordial conversation, but it wasn't anything personal.

When my brother died in 2012, Nick reached out to me by email. It was very sweet. We emailed back and forth, and somehow there was really a space of forgiveness and moving on with our lives in those emails, and I feel like we got complete. I do think that he's forgiven me. In an email, he said he'd moved on with his life. I believe he's in another relationship. I don't know if he's married, but he has moved on.

I'll always love him. We were together almost ten years. He's always going to have a place in my heart.

Leaving Nick was really hard. I not only lost him, but I also lost his family. When someone dies, you lose that person, but when I broke up that relationship, I lost everybody. I was Aunt Kathy to his niece and nephews, and all that stopped. That was very difficult.

If I had it to do over again, I wouldn't have married Nick. I do regret that. I still would have told him that I was questioning my sexuality as soon as I did, but I probably wouldn't have gotten married. I should not have done that—even though it looked like my only option at the time. I really wanted to work it out because I did love him, but looking back I should have postponed the wedding and sorted things out for myself before deciding whether to marry him or not.

—Kathy's Life Now—

Since leaving Nick, I've been in six relationships, all with women—one for about four and a half years. I'm in a relationship now that I believe will be life long. Sarah and I just really connect.

I do think the world is much different now. I have a friend whose daughter is gay. She's in college, she's out, and it's a beautiful thing that there's some space for people to be who they are—to be true to themselves. I never felt that there was a safe space like that for me.

It's a totally different world today in which people can deal with their sexuality at a much earlier age, and families are more supportive—not all of them, of course. I think the parents of my generation were more old school. For many of them, same-sex relationships are still not acceptable. It's still don't ask, don't tell.

Sarah's family is very Catholic, and she and I go there for Thanksgiving. She introduces me as Kathy—not as her girlfriend or her partner. They all know that we're a couple, but we don't talk about it. I've experienced that a lot in my relationships with women—the parents just won't talk about it. They don't ask, and we don't tell.

But for the most part, I find that people have been pretty accepting—at least they appear to be accepting. It's so interesting. It supports what I believe: that being authentic works.

It's funny because Nick thought that the Landmark seminar I was in when I came out was what turned me gay. I told him that wasn't what happened. All it did was have me look at my life and tell the truth, and for me the truth was that I'm a lesbian. That's me being authentic. If I hadn't told the truth, I would have lived a very suppressed life.

Chapter 3

Drew

Drew did not admit—even to himself—that he might be gay until he was thirty-six. He gradually came to realize it over a period of several years. He married Susan in 1989, and they had two children. Drew grew up with a physically abusive mother, and he married a girl just like mom. Susan and Drew separated after eleven years of marriage because of her physical and mental abuse. While they were still married, Drew started having sex with men. After leaving his wife, he had a six-year relationship with Karl. Drew works for a financial company and lives with his children. He wants to be in a long-term, committed relationship.

—Drew's Story—

It's not like I realized at some point that I'm gay. For me, this was a gradual process, like an awakening. It was a process of coming to terms with who I am in my own fashion. I didn't admit—even to myself—that I was gay until I was thirty-six.

There seem to be some people who are sure of their sexuality from a very young age. I was at an LGBT fundraising dinner recently, and the man across the table told me that his nine-year-old nephew just came out. How in the world can a nine year old understand himself well enough to declare he's gay? How? Sometimes I still don't know if I'm gay. At the age of nine, I can remember just being happy that I was nine. I know that our culture is more sexualized now. With TV and the Internet, kids are more aware of sex than I was and probably know more than I did.

People ask me if my being gay was what made me divorce my wife. It wasn't. The fact of the matter is it might have been a component, but it wasn't anywhere near a hundred percent of why I left Susan. I really wanted to have a good life with her, but unfortunately I didn't pick the right wife—or maybe she didn't pick the right husband. I don't know. All I know is that I divorced her because I couldn't live with her. Period.

—Marriage—

My marriage was hell. Susan was physically abusive. I want to be clear that, in talking about my relationship with her, I don't want to take Susan down. It's not my intention to do that or to punish her. But the truth was that she was abusive in all kinds of ways, and living with her was hell.

I realize that I played a significant part in all that drama. When I reflect back on the women in my life—Susan, my mother, my paternal-grandmother, the few girlfriends I've dated—they all had a mean streak. I seemed to be attracted to mean women—a lot like a moth drawn to a flame. If they didn't get what they wanted, they would go ballistic. Over time, I learned what to avoid so as not to piss them off. I learned to live my life so as not to get hit or screamed at or made wrong. It's a terrible way to live. I could never totally be myself and live the life I dreamed I would live.

Susan at no point ever apologized for what she did. She's never apologized for damaging our home, or leaving scratches and scars on my body, or breaking my toe that still aches every time it rains. It was as though violence was simply part of life for her, and she had no question that it was okay to live the life we were living. Never did she bring up that she thought the violence was wrong, or out of the ordinary, and maybe we should do something about it. Not once. I guess in her own way, she believed that I deserved to be punished for whatever she decided was a punishable offense.

Susan and I did just one couple's therapy session together, and she made lunch meat out of me in it. She told the therapist what she always told me—that everything was my fault, my problem, and my issue. We did only that one session because I saw that couple's therapy just wasn't going to work. Her attitude there was typical of her attitude about almost everything—it was her way or the highway.

There was no compromising with Susan. There was no discussion of what to do. She probably would say the same thing about me. When you get two stubborn people together, nothing ever changes. But I was willing at that point to get into what we needed to talk about. We simply weren't able to do it.

Even when I cheated on her in the end, I think it was partly spite and partly that I freaking needed some affection. Now I know that she's just not capable of nurturing and being affectionate. She's not even genuinely affectionate with our kids. It's just not her.

Susan and I didn't have the greatest sex life, but it wasn't because I didn't want to have sex with her. Some men I know who are gay just stopped having sex with their wives. That was never a problem for me. Sex was actually more of a problem for Susan. After we had children, her sex life just kind of died. This was long before she knew—and even before I knew—that I'm gay.

If I had grown up in a family that was not physically violent, I probably wouldn't have married Susan. I probably would have recognized the violence in her and that she was not who I wanted to spend my life with. But I didn't.

As far as divorce goes, I don't advocate it. I believe that divorce is an option if there are no other options. I mean I would have tried to work it out with her, but there was no working anything out with Susan. I wasn't in a situation where I could work it out. There were too many things out of my control, or out of my ability to change and make better.

Sometimes I wonder—if I'd married a woman who was capable of love and affection, would I still be married to her? Would my life be totally different? Would I have been able to manage what I needed to in myself and remain in the marriage? I don't know. But Susan wasn't like that. I wish I'd known that when I married her, but I didn't.

If I had married another woman and we'd had a good relationship, would I now be gay? I don't know, but I think I would have had to. I probably would have come to a better understanding of who I am, but a lot of the guys I meet are in what I would call "good marriages," and they still end up wanting to be with men instead.

So one way or another, I think I would have come out. But I couldn't talk to Susan in an adult way about it because she went from zero to off-the-charts drama in less than two seconds. There was no sitting down and having a conversation with her about anything. If I said anything she didn't want to hear or deal with, she'd go into a tailspin. So I became conditioned to not talking with her about things.

Knowing what I know now, maybe I could have handled myself differently, but that wasn't the case when Susan and I were together.

—Coming Out—

I started to change later in our marriage. Susan's abuse had reached a level that I knew, whether I was gay or straight, the marriage was over. I was done hiding scratch marks from her nails. I just hadn't figured out yet how to leave.

Around 1997, I started to use the Internet, which was still a relatively new tool. I had noticed that I'd started feeling attracted to men. I would stay in my office late at night doing research on gay married men to help me understand what was happening and what I should do. Mostly I was trying to figure out if there was something wrong with me.

I discovered websites where I could chat with other gay and bisexual men. There were so many gay married men out there. I found out that I was anything but alone.

At that time, the websites were not regionalized like they are today. I might meet someone to chat with who lived in North Carolina or California, and I spent hours doing that. The more I chatted, the more empowered I became.

I don't believe I was "living a lie," as some people put it. I was finally coming into my own. I was maturing and realizing who I am, and beginning to accept that I might be a gay man—not straight or even bisexual. I had signed up for a few websites and over a period of six months or so, I developed on-line friendships with several men. We discussed some pretty deep personal issues concerning our wives, our sexuality, our kids, and if we should come out.

In the entire time I'd known Susan, I'd never cheated on her. The thought had never even crossed my mind. And even though I was talking to these men, the distance kept us from meeting, and that was a good thing. Our conversations were enlightening for me and left me with plenty of time to think.

Around this time, I got into therapy at the suggestion of a doctor who asked me about some scratches on my neck. The doctor was mortified when I told her that Susan had scratched me in a rage. Her reaction made me realize I had to do something to change the direction my life was going. I saw a therapist by the name of Arthur for a short time. He was a Hasidic Jew who dressed in black and had long curls that dangled in front of his ears. He played with them compulsively.

Arthur and I never talked about my being gay. I was afraid to talk about that with him. I think I was afraid that if I spoke about being gay with anyone other than my on-line friends, it would make it real. I'd be letting the cat out of the bag and, once it was out, I might not be able to get it back in.

One day, as I was chatting on-line, I met Tom. Meeting Tom changed everything. He had just moved to Pittsburgh with his wife. It took me the longest time to get up the nerve to meet him in person. I really didn't want to face my fears, and I didn't want anything to happen.

We finally started meeting for lunch. We'd grab a pizza and sit outside his apartment and talk. I finally had a best friend who I could talk to about anything. We'd spend hours talking. Here I was, talking to someone who was in the exact same boat as I was, except that Tom didn't have children.

Soon he and I started getting together every Wednesday night to work out and play racquetball. Afterwards we'd go for a beer. Susan hated that I went out on Wednesday nights, but I declared it my time. One night after we had a beer, Tom and I found a secluded place and made out in his car. It felt so good to kiss another man. We continued to see each other for the next few months.

The next significant event for me on my path from straight to gay happened on a business trip to Washington, D.C. I was doing some lobbying work there for the national organization my company belongs to. I drove down a day early and looked around the gay district in Dupont Circle. I spent the next day on Capitol Hill and had dinner with a few people at a Thai restaurant right near where I'd been the night before. When dinner was over, I took off to get a cab back to my hotel.

When I got to the corner and turned to cross the street, a very handsome man was standing in front of me, and he said hello. He looked like Clark Kent—clean-cut and well dressed. He was a little taller than me, which made him intimidating, given that he wasn't more than a few inches from my face.

He smiled and said, "I was watching you." That flustered me even more. *When had there been time for him to watch me*? I'd just walked down the street. I was thinking, *Oh, my God, who is this guy*? I turned around and walked back up the street. Then I stopped and thought, *Wait a minute. Maybe there was something there.* I turned around. He was still staring at me. I was startled and abruptly turned to keep walking away from him. Then I stopped and looked back again. He was still there looking at me. That's when I walked back over to him. We talked, and after a while went back to my hotel room.

His name was David, and he was in D.C. on business. I had never had that kind of experience. David had seen me and followed me. He'd put himself in front of me when I went to cross the street. At the time, I wasn't aware of any of that, because I wasn't paying attention.

David and I began a sexual relationship that didn't last long, but meeting him was the perfect thing to happen at that point in my life. It put me on a path that eventually led me out of my marriage and into my life as a gay man. Being with him helped me see the degree to which my marriage wasn't working and realize that I needed to free up my life and take care of myself.

Susan found out that I'm gay when she went into my computer one afternoon and saw that I was visiting gay websites. She also discovered from my emails that I had been hanging out with Tom. She called me early that afternoon at work. When she told me what she'd found, I was euphoric at first, because I was finally out of the closet. But then I realized that I had to go home. That night, Susan beat the crap out of me. I was so battered I had to miss work for the next several days.

That was the last time that Susan—or anyone else—ever hit me.

—Gay Adolescence—

Looking back, I know I made the right choice in coming out, although it was difficult for me at the time. When I left Susan and started seeing David, he lived in Philadelphia. That was a good six-hour drive from Pittsburgh, and it was difficult for us to meet, particularly because I had two young children. It was the first time in my life that I got involved with someone outside my neighborhood. It was also difficult because at first I tried to make a committed relationship out of something that could never be a committed relationship.

A few months after David and I started seeing each other, he went on a cruise and had sex with someone. He came to see me afterward, and I couldn't deal with what he had done. I wasn't used to being treated that way. David had cheated on me. I'd only been in monogamous relationships up to that point.

Of course, I was blind to the fact that, by the end of our marriage, I was having sex with partners other than Susan. Hell, after I left Susan, I wasn't even being monogamous with David—even while I was upset with him for sleeping around. I was clearly having problems reconciling the reality of my new life with the values I'd always had about relationships, monogamy, and what I expected from my partner.

I wanted a committed relationship. I didn't want to sleep around, even though that was what I was doing. I obviously didn't know what I wanted.

I was seeing a therapist named Julie at that time. After I spoke with her, I was able to gain some perspective about what was happening to me. She told me that I was going through gay adolescence.

I had never heard the term before, but it described perfectly the point I was at in my life. On the one hand, I was a thirty-some-year-old man who wanted an adult relationship. On the other hand, I wasn't much different than a fifteen-year-old kid with hormones raging and a compulsive desire to make use of my new sexual identity. I was just coming out, and I had no clue how to act like an adult.

Wisely, Julie advised me that at that time of my life, I had no business being in a long-term exclusive relationship with anyone. It wouldn't be fair to my partner and wouldn't be fair to me. Soon after that, David and I ended our relationship, although we remain great friends.

—Drew's Life Now—

When I came out, I was afraid that coming out might ruin my life, but the opposite turned out to be true. Coming out made my life better because I could be myself. I didn't have to hide from myself any more.

Coming out changed my life in ways I couldn't have imagined. I stopped living as a victim. After Susan found out that I'm gay, things got even worse between us, and I knew I couldn't live with her any longer. I left Susan and went to court and won shared custody of my children. My son and daughter were only three and five at the time. They're now in their late teens and they both choose to live with me full time. I have a great relationship with my children. They mean the world to me.

Coming out to my family was easy. My parents were blue-collar people who lived in the suburbs. My father worked for a large manufacturing company, and my mother was a housewife. They struggled and scraped by all their lives. I was actually kind of surprised that there really never was an issue with my coming out to them. One day I was talking with my mother about something, and she asked me if I was gay. I said, "Ma, I like boys." That was it. That was pretty much all that happened. No one in my family had ever come out as gay, so there was really no precedent. I set the precedent.

I think that coming out in my mid-thirties may have had something to do with how easy it was for me. Who the hell was gonna tell me what to do at that point in my life? Who was gonna say that I shouldn't do this or I should do that? I think my parents saw that this was what I'd done, and they had to accept it.

I think if you're younger when you come out—say, sixteen or eighteen—your family may still try to influence your decisions. They may try to save you from yourself. My family knew that no matter what they said, I would do whatever I wanted.

About six months after I left Susan, I started dating Karl. I asked my therapist Julie how I should introduce him to my family. Her advice was to just show up with him. That's what I did. That's how I introduced Karl to my family—to my kids, my parents, and my other relatives. And it worked. Over time, my family came to really like him. I didn't make a big deal about having a boyfriend, and neither did anyone else.

In the years since I came out, I've become even more open about who I am. The more honest you are with people, the nicer they are to you.

People become disarmed when I share myself openly with them. One time, Susan told a group of parents whose kids played sports with my son that I'm gay. I know she did that to diminish me in their eyes, and I thought they might shun me after that. But they didn't. Not only did they not shun me, but it was my experience that they tried to support me. When you're genuine and honest and authentic with people, they reach out to you. I think we're all attracted to authenticity.

My relationship with Susan is very different now. I'm not trying to change her, but I don't allow her to abuse me anymore. I recently drove somewhere with her, and she started complaining almost as soon as she got in my car. I very calmly said, "I don't want to hear you complain about anything. You need to stop or get out." It was the most peaceful drive we'd had in years, although it didn't last. When I had to drive her somewhere again last week, she was as unpleasant as ever. I now do as little with Susan as I can.

Karl and I were together for six years. I really tried to make it work with him, but we had different agendas and different needs. We even went to couple's therapy for about six months because I wasn't willing to give up on it. But we couldn't make it work.

My friends who are in relationships … their relationships seem to be working pretty well. They have a good yin and yang. But for me and, I think, for many gay men, we're still looking.

Leaving my marriage was the right thing for me to do, although it was really hard at the time. I've never regretted it. In fact, I applaud it every day.

In the fourteen years since Susan and I parted, I've grown to love my life. I had no way of knowing then how happy I could be.

—Advice—

What Should You Do?

Life is too short to not be happy. Once you accept that you're gay, move forward with integrity and be at peace with yourself, however you decide to do that.

Children

You have to be honest with your kids. Hiding the fact that you're gay makes it harder on everyone. Honesty leads to a better relationship with your children.

Get Support

Most people don't have much consciousness about themselves and their lives, and it makes such a difference when you do. I'm not sure how to suggest that you do that, other than to say that it made a big difference for me to go to a therapist. Nobody wants to go to a therapist ... but, man, do they call you out on your shit.

Julie, the therapist I saw after I left Susan, would make a little comment about something I was talking about, and it would leave me questioning myself. *You mean that's not what I should be doing?* She usually wouldn't tell me what I should or shouldn't do. She would just allow me to figure it out for myself as we kept talking. Other times she would have suggestions for me that made perfect sense for me but that I never would have thought of on my own.

Julie put things in perspective for me. There are many things that are not good in the gay world, and there are many good things too. That's true in the straight world. It's true in life. But when you're in the gay world, you don't think that anything else exists, because the two worlds don't really come together.

I would say to Julie that it's just that way in the gay world, and she would say, "Oh, no, it's that way in both worlds, but this is the world you're in right now." She always put things into perspective for me. She was there for me as I was going through my divorce and my custody battle with Susan. I would email Julie, and she'd respond to me—any time. She coached me through it all.

I would not be in as good shape as I am today if I hadn't worked with Julie. She really set the stage for my recovery. Julie was a lesbian who had been married to a man, had a daughter, and came out. What better situation could I have been in than to have a therapist who had already been through what I was going through?

Chapter 4

Trudy

When she was only nine or ten years old, Trudy knew that she was attracted to other girls. Her mother told her that she would go to hell, and agreed to send her to a convent boarding school. Trudy loved it there. An incident at school convinced her that the path she needed to take in life was to go to college, get married, and have children. That was the path she took. After she finished college, Trudy married Rich. They were married for eleven years when Rich left her for another woman. Trudy was living in a small town in rural Ohio, going to graduate school, working full time, and raising two young boys. She dated a few men, and then committed to a year of celibacy. After that year, at the age of thirty-nine, Trudy was clear that she is a lesbian. She moved to Pittsburgh, and two years later began a relationship with Jan, the woman she is still with. Trudy is now sixty-six and retired. She used to be a therapist and the executive director of a non-profit.

—Trudy's Story—

I knew I was attracted to females when I was about nine or ten, and I got a lot of negative messages about that. My mother told me that I was going to go to hell. I can't say that my mother knew exactly what was going on with me, but she suspected. Then one day she caught me fooling around with some other girls.

I had told my parents that I wanted to go to a boarding school. I wanted to go so I wouldn't have to deal with boys, because they made me so uncomfortable at that time in my life. After my mother caught me with the other girls, I was sent to a convent boarding school for high school.

It turned out to be a wonderful experience. The nuns there were fabulous. It was a small school. There were a hundred girls total. Probably a third were boarders and the rest were day students, so there were only a small number of boarders.

An incident in the dorms one night changed my life. It probably saved my life. Thirty boarders went to sleep that night, and when we woke up the next morning, there were only twenty-eight of us. It leaked out that two of the girls were caught in bed together, and they were forced to leave during the night. Their parents were called to come and get them in the middle of the night and to take all their stuff with them. The next morning it was like they didn't exist—like they hadn't even been there. That was a really strong message for me. That was back in '62 or '63, when being gay wasn't something anybody talked about openly. It just wasn't discussed.

That incident cemented my belief that I would go on to college and then get married and have kids. And that's what I did. When I finished college, I did some work with VISTA in rural Virginia and then went back to Youngstown, Ohio, which was the area where I'd spent my high school and college years. I really wanted babies and in 1970, you didn't have babies unless you were married.

—Marriage—

In Youngstown, I reconnected with Rich, a guy I'd dated some in college. Not long afterward, Rich and I got married. It all happened so fast. I wasn't pregnant, but it was a fast marriage. His family was from a rural part of Ohio. They had deep roots there.

I was attracted to their rootedness because my dad was a metallurgical engineer for a large corporation and every two and a half years, he'd get promoted and we'd move. We'd lived in northeastern Pennsylvania; then Oakridge, Tennessee (that was back when it was still a secret city); Niagara Falls; Long Island; West Virginia; Thailand; New Jersey; and then Ohio. After my boys were both out of high school, I moved to Pittsburgh. But that was much later. When I initially reconnected with Rich, part of my attraction to him was his family history in this one place, which was very appealing to me.

I can't say that I loved Rich. It was more that I loved the idea of being married and I wanted to have kids, and Rich seemed to be a good choice—but I was not madly in love with him. Of course, I never talked to him about my attraction to women. I never talked to anybody about that.

Was it a good marriage? That's a hard question for me to answer. I don't know. There were things that worked about it, and other things that didn't work. I can say that we were never clear with each other about our expectations, and we were always tripping over that.

Here's just a simple example. I fixed rice for dinner one night, and Rich said, "Finally—I didn't think you were ever going to make rice. I love rice." He had never said that to me before that he loved rice. I guess we'd been married several years at that point. It was a minor detail but also a perfect example of his and my inability to express our expectations. It's how we both were.

Another thing that didn't work between us was sex. I wasn't a good sexual partner for him. I did what I had to do, but I didn't do it enough to make him happy. You can only fake so much.

We were married for eleven years and had two sons when Rich got involved with another woman. He left me. I wasn't surprised that he left me. What I didn't expect was the level of dishonestly he displayed. That was surprising to me and very hurtful. I'm someone who would rather be punched than lied to.

After he left, I spent the next several years trying to figure out who the heck I was while trying to raise two boys—they were eight and five when Rich and I separated—plus finish graduate school and work full time.

—Coming Out—

I didn't come out for a while after that. Rich and I had lived in a small town in rural Ohio, not far from the town where his family lived. After we separated, we both continued to live in that area. He spent every other weekend with the boys, and on those weekends I would date. I dated a few men, mostly a lot of losers.

After a year of that, I committed to a year of celibacy. I wasn't going to do anything with anybody—I didn't care whether it was male, female, or a duck. I just wasn't going to do it. I came out of that year very clear that I'm gay and that it was okay for me to be gay. Well, I shouldn't go so far as to say that it was okay, but I knew that I was a lesbian and that that's where my attractions were. So at the age of thirty-nine, I started to date women. It was great.

It was a little tricky with the boys, and Rich and I were not communicating well at that time. We are now, but we weren't speaking then, and I was concerned that he could use my being a lesbian against me in court. That scared me, so that's why I would date—whether it was a man or a woman—only when the boys weren't around. That was every other weekend. It allowed me the best of both worlds: I got to be a mom when my sons were with me, and I got to be single when they were with their father.

I was in graduate school to become a therapist, and one of the people I came out to was my thesis advisor, who was also a therapist. I told her that I was pretty sure I was gay. She said, "Oh, no, you can't be gay." She didn't want anybody to be gay. It was that simple. Until 1973, homosexuality was included as a disorder in the *Diagnostic and Statistical Manual of Mental Disorders*. That was the environment I came out in.

In 1991, I moved to Pittsburgh. I was in my mid-forties. One of the reasons I moved was because I had some family here. Also I had been working as a therapist in Ohio, and my clients included most of the very small lesbian community in the town where I lived. I couldn't date clients, so my dating options were pretty slim there. In general, I just felt constricted in Ohio, and I wanted to get out of there. So I decided to try Pittsburgh.

I was dating someone from Pittsburgh when I moved here. We were together about three years. After that relationship ended, I started a relationship with Jan, the woman I'm still with.

—Jan—

I met Jan when I first moved to Pittsburgh. I was clinical director at a non-profit agency, and Jan worked for the county in a funding position for the type of treatment we offered. She and I developed a professional relationship, which grew into a friendship, and that grew into the relationship we have today. We've been together as a couple since 1993.

You would think that we're a married couple, but we're not. I would have gotten married, but Jan is clear that she wants full legal rights before she gets married. We've talked about taking a tour of the country and making a video in every place where we could get married, and coming back to Pittsburgh and filming ourselves being turned away from the marriage license window at the courthouse to illustrate how unjust it is.

But I think that full legal rights are not that far away. I'm not sure at this point that it benefits us to get married. A friend of ours has been talking recently about some new information she has that gay couples need to think carefully about marriage because there can be certain financial disadvantages to being married. For instance, if I had to go into a nursing home and if Jan and I are married, she'd be responsible for the bill. If we weren't married, the state would pay. So there are all kinds of pros and cons. When you can't have something, you want it, whereas if that taboo isn't there, you can choose whether you want it or not.

My commitment to Jan goes far beyond a marriage license. What we have is so different from what I experienced in my marriage that I'm not really comfortable with the word *marriage*. It doesn't seem to fit for me. I'd like to find a word that fits us.

I can't imagine anything more committed than what Jan and I have. It seems ludicrous to put that commitment in some box of a word.

Jan is an absolute joy. Oh, my God, she's so funny, and she's so smart.

—Trudy's Life Now—

I retired a few months ago, and I have a lot more freedom now that I don't have the responsibility of running an agency on my shoulders. It's a tremendous responsibility. Now I get to do a lot of traveling with Jan—she travels around the state doing trainings and things like that. I also get to go to California more often to see my grandsons.

I couldn't figure out why I decided to retire when I did because I loved my job and I had a good salary and a fabulous staff, but I had this voice screaming at me, You have to retire. *You have to retire.* So I did. I retired last year, and soon afterward a dear friend of mine was diagnosed with cancer. I spent most of my first year of retirement caring for her. So apparently that's why I retired. It was an amazing gift to be with her.

My relationship with Rich … I wouldn't call it good, but we're civil with each other. We talk on a regular basis about our sons, so that's been helpful. He's still with the woman that he left me for, and they live in the same town where he and I used to live. I have family there, so I'm down there a lot and I run into him.

The only other thing that I would add is that I find it much more comfortable to be sixty-six and to have lived through all these changes that I've lived through. It's easy to forget the sort of harriedness I used to feel inside when all that was happening and I couldn't quite figure it out. For people my age, coming out has not always been a graceful process. Having that behind me is wonderful, as is being settled and happy in my life.

—Advice—

What Should You Do?
I think men are better at having non-emotional sexual relationships than women are. And with the Internet now, men don't even have to go to bars. It's dangerous. HIV and syphilis are on the upswing again. Pittsburgh is having an epidemic of syphilis—among gay men in the city and heterosexual couples in a small town about twelve miles south of Pittsburgh.

It's a very different world now than the one I grew up in. Things are very fluid today. People can get in touch easily with other people—and nobody else needs to know they've been in touch. The opportunities for dishonesty have grown exponentially, and that's too bad.

What's interesting is that the opportunity for honesty is also growing. It seems that as gay marriage is becoming more common, more people are coming out, and to me that's a lot about telling the truth.

Talk with Your Spouse
My advice is to talk with your partner. Be honest with your partner. If you can't be honest in a relationship, then it's not a good relationship, and

you ought to think about getting out. If you can't be honest with the person you're married to, who can you be honest with? Whether your attraction to someone other than your spouse is heterosexual or homosexual, if you can't talk honestly with your partner, why be in that relationship?

Children

I think you have to be clear about expectations—particularly when children are involved. If your relationship isn't working and you're both unhappy, but you can manage it for your kids in a way that's not destructive, then I think you should stay until the kids are out of the home. If you can't do that, then you need to be honest with each other and talk about it. It's deceitfulness that's damaging, I think, to the kids and the partners and everybody else who's involved.

Coming Out

I think you have to be respectful of your family—whether it's your parents, kids, brothers and sisters, whatever. The expectation that everybody in your world is going to say "Oh, goody" when you come out is really unrealistic. You need to have respect for people, and you need to have an understanding of time and the time it will take for people to be okay with who you're telling them you are, because they've lived their whole life believing you were somebody else.

It really takes time and patience, and often people don't have that when they first give themselves the freedom to be who they are. They don't feel patient. They want everything right away. *Oh, this is wonderful. I want to live in it full time.* Well, you already have a life, and there are people in that life who have not made this transition with you, so it's very important to be thoughtful and considerate and careful. You don't want to break or damage relationships in a way that they can't be repaired. So my advice is to be thoughtful and considerate.

I never did come out to my parents. No. No. No. My parents were both active alcoholics. My brother knew, and my aunt—who was the kindest person in the world—was pretty sure. But I didn't say anything to my parents. They met Jan, and they knew she was in my life all these years, but it was just never spoken, and the relationship I had with them was not one that encouraged me to tell them who I am.

A lot of times, people just need time to come to terms with your coming out. If they love you, they probably will. They're going to come to love you as you are, but it sometimes takes time for people to get used to change.

People don't always deal with change well, and this is a change. Oh, my God, yeah! When I talk with people who are just coming out, I always say, "Think about how long it took you to figure this out."

Chapter 5

Gene

Unlike Drew and Kathy, Gene always knew he was gay, but being gay didn't stop him from falling in love with Casey. He met her when he was sixteen, and they became close friends. Compared to her family, Gene was from the wrong side of the tracks. "Casey took me under her wing," he said, "and made me who I am today." After dating for ten years, they decided to get married. While they were engaged, Casey asked Gene if he was gay. He was afraid to tell her the truth, but he wasn't willing to lie to her. He told Casey the truth. Casey's mother recommended that Gene should speak with a priest, who recommended a therapist. While in therapy, Gene realized he "didn't want to be gay" anymore. He wanted to marry Casey. So Gene and Casey went ahead with the wedding. They were married for twelve years, have one daughter, and are now divorced. They are still best friends. Now forty-eight, Gene has been with Jake since 2001. He works as a project manager.

—Gene's Story—

I guess I've known since I was a kid that I'm gay. I didn't describe it that way. I just always gravitated toward the girls in the neighborhood and in school. I always knew that I was different from other boys, but never knew really what it meant.

I met Casey, who eventually became my wife, when I was sixteen. I was a busboy at a restaurant, and she was a waitress. I was drawn to her, and we became friends. Compared to her family, I came from a family from the other side of the tracks. My parents were divorced, and we were poor. Casey's family was different. Her dad was educated. He was a schoolteacher. She took me under her wing and made me who I am today.

—Coming Out—

Casey and I dated for ten years and decided to get married. At some point during our engagement, she sat me on the couch one day to talk. Casey knew that something was different about the way I acted and reacted with her. I was different from other guys. So she asked me, "What's going on? What's bothering you?" Finally she just came out and asked, "Are you gay?" I was afraid to tell her the truth. I didn't want to risk losing her. But I couldn't lie to her. So I told her the truth, "Yes, I'm gay." She wanted to know if I'd had relationships with men, and I told her I had. I answered all her questions.

After that conversation, at the recommendation of Casey's mom, I went to see a priest for a while. Ultimately the priest said, "There's really nothing I can do for you, so let me recommend a therapist." After that, I went to a therapist for years.

In the meantime, Casey and I decided to get married because I didn't want to be gay. I wanted to be married to her and to have children.

—Marriage—

We were married for twelve years. I loved Casey, and to this day we're still best friends. But loving each other and being best friends weren't enough to keep our marriage alive.

It got to a point in our relationship where we weren't having sex.

We were just living as brother and sister. I think it started shortly after our daughter Bennett was born, which was in '94. I just wasn't drawn to Casey sexually anymore. She was trying. She would make advances, but I would always find an excuse to not have sex.

Finally she came to terms with it and said, "You need to go. You need to live your life." As hard as that was to do, she did it, which I give her credit for, because I probably would have just continued to live that way. I moved out in 2001, and we got divorced the following year. The divorce was amicable. There was nothing that was mean or harsh about it. We stayed friends through it. Our main concern was the well-being of our daughter. Bennett was and continues to be our number-one priority.

—Gene's Life Now—

I care for Casey so I'm always trying to find ways to help her. It's so funny. When we met, I was the shy one, and she was more outgoing. Since then, our worlds have reversed, and now I'm more verbal and outgoing and she's more introverted. She has very few friends. Even when I joke with her, she still doesn't know how to take me, after all this time. We've been friends since 1981. At the core, we've been best friends all through our adult lives.

She still sometimes takes offense, even though my goal is never to hurt her. Like I said, I'm always looking for ways to try to help her. For instance, she has two dogs and she doesn't have much control over them. They're like her kids. I'm always telling her she needs to train her dogs because they control her life. I always voice my opinion with her because I feel as though I can, and sometimes that ticks her off. That's also the way it was when we were married. Sometimes she thinks I need to mind my own business.

In addition to not having many friends, Casey also hasn't dated in a long time. Early on, after I moved out, she was fixed up with somebody and they dated for a while and planned to get married. I advised her against marrying him. I knew that getting married to that guy was the biggest mistake she could make. He was doing nothing for her or my daughter. I thought, if they get married, it's just going to get worse. He was living with his sister, and Casey was driving him home at midnight. There were things like that I knew, so I spoke up about it, and since then she hasn't dated. People try to fix her up, but she says she has no desire to date.

I moved in with Jake in 2001, soon after Casey and I separated. We met through mutual friends. Jake is wonderful. He loves my daughter. He's fine with us going on vacation with Casey and Bennett. There are a lot of guys who wouldn't do that.

We've all benefited from this relationship in different ways, without question. Jake's parents died in 2007. His mom passed in February and his dad in June. Their house needed to be cleaned out. Jake has an older sister who wasn't able to help. He and I were planning to clean it out, and it looked overwhelming. Then Casey and Bennett offered to help us. The four of us cleared that entire house out and moved out all their possessions.

I'm not into going to bars. I did that at one time in my life. Now I'm more of a family man than a gay man. I'm a homebody. Jake's toned down a lot since we've been together. He came out late—when he was thirty-eight—and he was that kid in the candy store for a while. I was part of his kid-in-the-candy-store phase, and I had to have a lot of patience with him.

Before he came out, Jake wasn't married, but he dated a lot of women. Early in our relationship, he had an issue with saying he was gay. He'd say, "I'm bisexual," and I'd tell him, "You are not a bisexual man." I would ask him how many times he'd looked at a woman that day. He'd always say, "Never." I still look at women and I love women for who they are, but I'm not bisexual. I adore women. I think women are beautiful. Their bodies are beautiful. But I have no desire to be with a woman.

Jake has now come to grips with being a gay man, but he's still not as openly gay as I am. He works at a casino, and all the little cocktail servers think he's just the cutest thing—even though they call him "grandpa" because he's a silver-top. He doesn't divulge the fact that he's gay, whereas I do. At work, people know I'm gay because I fought for domestic-partner benefits for Jake. He's not like that.

I'm so fortunate to have the life that I have. I have Jake. I have a great relationship with Casey and Bennett. I have fifteen nieces and nephews. I still get along well with my former mother- and father-in-law, who are in their eighties. Jake and I just spent a couple of hours with them yesterday. They love me, and they love Jake.

Casey's parents didn't want her with me initially. I was the first person ever to stand up to her mother. She was always the ruler of the roost, and when Casey and I got engaged, her mother cried. She was not happy, and it was very tough on Casey at the time. So Casey and I sat down at her parents' house. They didn't want to hear anything I had to say. Finally I got up in her mom's face and told her that I was in love with her daughter, and I didn't know who she thought she was to say that I couldn't be with Casey. From that day on, we've had a better understanding of each other. Today we get along beautifully. For our holiday dinners, Jake and I cook for thirty to forty people and that always includes Casey and her family.

People have been much more accepting than I thought they would be. Even when we were getting a divorce and we told Casey's parents, they were never mean or ugly to me. I was leaving their daughter, and I never saw them disrespect me. But I had always respected them.

I'm fortunate and I know it. I have to say I've never had a negative experience with being gay. That's why I'm not afraid to say that I'm gay. I am a gay man. I am who I am. You either like me for who I am or you don't. If you find out I'm gay and you don't like me, that's your problem.

—Advice—

What Should You Do?

If you're a man who's married to a woman and having sex with other men, I'd say first of all you're lying to yourself. Take a long look in the mirror and know that you may end up living with regret for the rest of your life if you keep on the path you're on.

I have a friend who was into the bar scene and ended up becoming HIV positive. He now has to live with the consequences of his actions. Men can be stupid. They just don't think. My grandmother always said, "Men think with their dicks." Pardon my French, but that's just what men tend to do.

Coming Out

I have another friend who's fifty-three years old, he has three adult children, and he's divorced. He's now in a relationship with a forty-year-old man. He's always at this guy's house. They vacation together. They do almost everything together. Yet he refuses to tell his kids that he's gay. I've told him that his kids do in fact know—they're not stupid. I've told him how much easier his life would be if he were to come out to his kids. Coming out makes life a whole lot easier, without question.

Chapter 6

Erin

Erin met Jack in college. They fell in love and were married in 1971, and within a few years had two daughters. But Erin and Jack had different values, and the gap between them only widened over time. Their marriage lasted eleven years. After they separated, when she was in her mid-thirties, Erin came to realize that she is a lesbian. Ten years after she came out, she met the love of her life. She and Amy were together for fifteen years until Amy died in 2007. Erin is now opening up to the possibility of being in a relationship again. She is a university professor.

—Erin's Story—

I was in my mid-thirties when I first got into a relationship with a woman. But that probably wasn't the first time I was attracted to a woman. When I look back … probably not. I went to a women's college, and there were lots of really close friendships. I think that changes one's perspective. Before that, in high school, we had Big Sisters, and I remember seeing my Big Sister in a play where she was playing a guy. I thought, *Wow—she's really cute*, but I justified it to myself by saying that she was playing a man. That was probably the only clear time in my past that I remember being attracted to a female. I think for women attraction and caring about people get mixed together. That's why it's harder for many women to know where they stand.

—Marriage—

Jack and I met in college, and we got married in 1971. We were both in love, and he was a nice Irish Catholic guy so my family was happy. His family was a little more upper-middle class than we were.

At first we were pretty happy. Two years later our daughter Eve was born, and the following year we had Stephanie. Having children changed things between Jack and me. His expectations changed. From his perspective, I had two choices: I could stay home and take care of my husband, my children, and my house; or I could go to work and also take care of my husband, my children, and my house. That created some pressure between us.

We were young, and those were the days when you had children quickly. In fact, if a married woman didn't get pregnant within two years, everybody assumed there was something wrong.

After Stephanie was born, I stayed home for four months and then went back to work part-time. After I'd been working a year, I was offered a fellowship to get my doctorate, and I took it.

I had my hands full. Luckily, my girls were easy. I often studied from midnight to 2 a.m. because that's the only time I had. I lived on four to five hours of sleep a night for years.

Our marriage lasted until 1982.

All in all, I think we had a good marriage for the first two years, and then it became problematic. Jack wanted me to be more traditional, and that just wasn't going to happen. We developed different values. We got married young, and you don't always develop your values that early. And that was such a time of change—lots of things were changing. The women's movement created so many options for women.

I was in a women's group and involved in a lot of women's issues. From my perspective, there were a lot of women looking at things differently. That was really exciting to live through.

Through all of it, Jack and I continued to grow apart.

I left him for all the reasons I've talked about and also because of Eve and Stephanie. I knew that I could figure out how to deal with it all, but I didn't want them growing up in that environment. There was tension in our house, but also the expectation that I would live more traditionally in a way that I didn't think was appropriate. And then Jack would be angry when I didn't do that. Why put your children through that? Why keep somebody in that situation when it's not going to work—especially a female?

Our divorce ended up being amicable, and… yeah, for the most part it was.

If I had it to do over, would I marry Jack again? Probably not. Oh, isn't it hard to look backward? I probably wouldn't marry him—not that he wasn't a good person. But I don't think we really knew each other very well. I don't think we're taught very well how to pick partners. What I probably would have done is wait longer.

—Coming Out—

I realized that I'm gay when I was about thirty-four and I was separated from Jack. Through my work, I'd met a few gay men and lesbians, and I was sometimes invited to their social and political gatherings—like if people were going to a lesbian bar to support a particular cause, I sometimes went too. That was the age of feminism, so a number of my friends who are straight also did that because it was a way to be together with other women.

Before I got involved with a woman though, I waited until Jack and I were divorced because I didn't want to risk losing custody of my daughters. So it wasn't until after our divorce that I came out to Jack.

It was all so ridiculous. Even before I came out, I was pretty well out, given that I'd been a spokesperson for gay and lesbian rights for years.

When I did come out to Jack, he was disparaging. "I heard you're one of those …" he said. "How come you always have to be so different?" Most of my friends weren't surprised when I came out. But Jack and I really didn't know each other well, even after being married for eleven years. A lot of his reaction may have been that he was hurt—hurt that I had left, and hurt that I had made choices that looked like he wasn't okay. How could he have competed?

I ended up meeting a woman who was pretty aggressive—not in a negative way, just more aggressive in terms of pushing herself into my life. After a while, being with her felt like a comfortable place to be. It felt natural.

I have this theory that when you're not completely open to something new, the people who get in are the ones who don't pay attention to you saying "No, thank you." That's because the people who are sensitive wait to be invited, and the ones who aren't very sensitive just jump in and get close before you know they're there.

I also think that when it's with another woman, it's different because it's not something you're expecting. If a man had been getting that close to me, I would have had barriers up, but it just never occurred to me what was happening with her until I was in the middle of it. That wasn't a bad thing. It was a good way for me to figure out where I was and what I wanted— without being afraid of hurting feelings, because she was pretty tough.

She was more on the butch or masculine side. I think that's often what people do when we're making a change like that. We go to an extreme. That's what I did. She and I saw each other for about six months. It just didn't work. We were in different places. And as you may have heard, most of the time the person that you come out with is not the person that you end up staying with.

I think that's similar to what happens in heterosexual relationships— that you usually don't stay with the person you start seeing right after a breakup. A lot of this is not so different between straight and gay relationships. What's different is the stigma attached to gay relationships. But otherwise, the feelings are very close, and even the behavior is very close.

With men, it's a little different, I think, because they don't have the same boundaries that women do—particularly where you have two people who get together right away.

It's very interesting learning how to pick differently. I think as heterosexuals we look for somebody different from the person we're unhappy with—even diametrically opposed to that person—and that's not who we want either.

I met Karen shortly after that. We were in a relationship for ten years. It was a good relationship for a while. She was somebody who was more masculine in many ways, including the it's-not-my-job-to-take-care-of-the-house kind of masculine. After my marriage ended, I thought I would never put up with that from a man again. It never occurred to me that I'd put up with it from a woman. I just didn't expect it. She was a good person, four or five years younger than me, and she'd never lived on her own. I think it didn't work between us because we were in such different places. As time went on, that just wasn't going to fly.

My daughters were living with me then. I had full custody. They saw their dad every other weekend and every Tuesday night.

—Amy—

Not long after Karen and I parted, I met Amy.

She and I met in 1992, when I was forty-four, and we were together for fifteen years before she died. She was a therapist. When we met, she lived in a small town in northeastern Pennsylvania, and I was living in Philadelphia, so we had a long-distance relationship for about five years.

Amy and I had a really good relationship. It was an equal relationship. She was very smart, very skilled, and also much more social than I am. We were both pretty strong-willed, particularly after having raised families of our own. Like me, she had been married and she had a child.

In 1997, she left her small town and moved to Philadelphia. I didn't seriously consider moving there. Besides the fact that I had a job in Philadelphia, it would have been much harder for us in Amy's small town for a couple reasons. It was harder to be out in such a small town. Also, she had back problems and had to have several major surgeries, so she wanted to live close to decent medical care.

She started a private practice in Philadelphia while she was going back and forth. She would see clients there every Monday. Her clients loved her. She did really good work with them, and her social skills with clients were excellent. But she was outspoken, and people either really loved her or really didn't like her. Mostly they loved her.

She died in 2007. Amy was an athlete, and she had heart problems. She was running one afternoon by the river, and she had a heart attack—but she didn't realize she'd had a heart attack, so she didn't go to the hospital right away. I don't know if it would've made a difference if she had.

After a time she did go, and she called me at my office. It was a Saturday, and I wasn't there. By the time I got her message and went to the hospital, she had died. She'd had a massive heart attack, and they couldn't save her. She was gone pretty quickly. For me, it was like walking off a cliff.

There were over three hundred people who signed in at her service. I didn't expect that—I didn't even know she knew three hundred people. My daughter Eve was the one who said to me, "Mom, you have to get a bigger place."

So many people spoke at her service. It was amazing—particularly, I think, for her family and hopefully for her daughter. People from all walks of life spoke about her and the difference she had made in their lives—CEOs of companies, the guy who took care of our computer, our friends. They all spoke. But it … it's still such a big loss.

It's amazing how people loved her. I hadn't been back to the mechanic who used to take care of our car—I had to take it to the dealer instead for a while. So it was a few years after Amy died before I went back to him again. When I walked into his garage, the first thing he said to me was, "I was just thinking about Amy." That happened a lot. I'd walk into a place or see somebody on the street, and they'd tell me how much they missed her. It's pretty wonderful. She was well respected—we were—in many places.

—Erin's Life Now—

I moved back to Pittsburgh a few years ago. I'm not in a relationship now. I haven't met anybody that I've wanted to be with. Amy's sort of hard to replace.

My life is pretty full. I still work part time, I have good friends, I'm involved in interesting activities, and I travel a lot.

Eve lives in California, so she's pretty far away. She went to college there and fell in love with it. Stephanie lives in D.C. Aside from the typical mother-daughter things, I have a good relationship with both of them. I see them each three or four times a year. It's nice. We talk regularly.

I think in some ways, since Amy died, traveling is a way for me to keep busy, and I think I'm coming to a place where I still like to travel and I will for awhile, but I'm more open to not being quite as busy. When you're busy, you can't let people in as far. There's a cost to being busy. You don't necessarily see opportunities. One of my friends asked me if someone had tried to fix me up. I said, "No, I don't think they had." She asked, "Would you have noticed?"

In some ways, it would be nice to have a partner again. I have a nice life, and I have people I can count on, so it's a pretty good life right now. I went through a very brief period last year—because somebody challenged me—where I thought I'd like to have a partner again. Then I realized that the concept of being in a relationship was good, but there wasn't anybody I was interested in. Somebody will probably show up when I stop thinking about it.

—Advice—

What Should You Do?

Some people choose to stay together in a straight marriage even though one of them is gay. If they can make that decision well and both people know what's going on, it can work. Love has lots of different faces. And sexuality is nice, but it's not the only way to love somebody. Some people are better friends than partners. As my daughter said when she was little, "What's wrong with loving people?"

Talk with Your Spouse

My advice for someone who's in a straight marriage and questioning if they are straight is to talk with your spouse. Of course, that's really general advice and it depends on the relationship. I wouldn't suggest doing that if you're in a violent relationship. But in general, I'd suggest that you talk with your spouse.

Children

Talk to your kids when you're sure what you want to do. They don't need to be part of the negotiations, but if you're a woman who's leaving your husband, your kids need to know that—especially if you're leaving to be with somebody else. You need to talk with your kids before that point.

Get Support

If you're considering leaving a straight marriage because you think you might be gay or lesbian, I suggest you talk with a therapist or another professional about it, or talk with a friend that you trust. Talk with somebody where you don't have to worry about what they think of you—because if you're willing to talk with people about it, you'll be less closeted, and you'll have to deal with it more.

Chapter 7

Ben

When Ben was a teenager, he was interested in guys but never felt that he had an option to do anything about his interest. He married Marin in 1991, when he was thirty years old. "I loved her then, and I still love her," he explained. Prior to getting married, he had one sexual encounter with a man. Afterward, he put that part of himself "on a shelf"—as he described it—until his mid-thirties, when he started traveling for work and experimenting with having sex with men. Over time, his sexual relationship with Marin waned. The two have been separated since 2006. Now fifty-two years old, Ben is an engineer. At the time of this interview, he was in a relationship with Tom. Their relationship has since ended, and Ben is now involved with another man.

—Ben's Story—

I can't give you a black-and-white answer about when I realized I was gay. One of the things I've learned in talking to other gay men is that some men say they knew without a doubt that they were gay at a very early age. That wasn't true for me. Did I question it at a young age? Probably in my early teens I did, but whether it was about being gay or not, I don't know. I mean I noticed that I was attracted to men. I was into sports, and when I'd shower or be in the locker room, I'd find myself looking at other guys.

I had fooled around sexually with guys when I was younger—twelve or thirteen. There were books and studies—things like the Kinsey report, things that you hear about or see in a magazine—about how that's normal for adolescent males. You know, it was normal to experiment, so I just chalked it up to experimentation.

As a kid, I fooled around with both boys and girls—with guys my age when I was younger and with girls when I was a teenager. As an adolescent, my focus was female one hundred percent. I didn't date a lot in high school. People often think that I was popular when I was younger—that I dated a lot of girls. But I was never really popular, and I didn't date a lot in high school or in college. When I did date, however, I dated girls, and I had sex with girls.

I would look at guys, I'd be interested, but being a teenager and being in Pittsburgh, I didn't really think I had an option to do anything about my interest in guys. If there had been more opportunity or if things had been more open, I don't know—I might have taken the chance.

Right after I graduated from college, I went to San Francisco to visit friends, and they took me around the city. One of the places we went was the Castro District. Gay men were very open there. I saw stuff happen in the Castro District at a Friday afternoon happy hour that, if anybody had tried anything like that in Pittsburgh at that time, complete strangers would have beaten them up to where they'd have to be hospitalized. So when I came back home, I probably continued looking at other men, I might have thought about having sex with men, but it was impossible for me to even consider myself gay.

A few years later, when I was twenty-four or twenty-five, I had a sexual encounter with a guy one time, and then that was it. That was prior to getting married. The whole thing—I'm not going to say it freaked me out.

It's just that I wasn't prepared. It was a lot to deal with, being from a straight world and having gay sex. It was a lot to wrap my brain around. I'm sure that most gay men don't decide one day that they're gay and go out and have sex that night. I'm sure there's some transition before they have sex, and I didn't have that transition.

The guy I had sex with—I'd known him for more than ten years. We worked together in the summers and were on a ski trip. He'd gone through an amazing evolution. When I first met him, he was a very outgoing, gregarious person and was staunchly anti-gay. He thought homosexuals were horrible, bad people. By the second year we worked together, he'd become a born-again Christian and was proselytizing against homosexuality. He would talk about how being gay was wrong and horrible and on down the list. In year number three, he came back to the job, and he was dating another man. He was openly out. From that point on, he was gay. He's a very good guy, all in all. That was his evolution, I guess, from denial and resistance to acceptance.

That was my one sexual encounter with a man as an adult before I got married. Afterward, I put my attraction to men on the shelf and left it there until my mid-thirties.

—Marriage—

I'd known Marin since I was nineteen. I met her and we started dating at the end of my sophomore year in college. Pretty much we dated consistently after that. I mean I never dated another woman after I met her.

I loved Marin. Was I in love? That's not an easy question for me, because it goes back to the issue of sexuality. You can love someone, but I think to be in love—that's been a challenge for me to define. I loved Marin. I still love her. I still care for her. We still have a very good relationship. We still talk daily.

Marin and I got married about eleven years after we met. In my relationship with my wife, we had sex, and we had intimacy regarding how we felt about things. The only thing I didn't talk about with her was my sexual attraction to men. That did create a kind of barrier between us.

I'm really glad that we were married. Absolutely. I think that in general men have a challenge in defining love in relationships. I think that's especially true of men who have never had a relationship with a woman and have never been taught how to be in relationship with a woman. I think that's a missing component for many men. It's one thing to date a man—to go out—but that's not the same thing as a relationship. There aren't sacrifices and choices in just dating as there are in a true relationship.

I have a friend whom I've talked with about this. He has clear priorities in his life, clearly defined priorities and expectations from a relationship, how you grow together within a relationship, and how a relationship is about *we* not *me*. He and I agree that it's hard to find that in the gay community, especially with guys who have never had children, have never had a relationship with a woman, and have never had to make sacrifices for anyone other than themselves.

I have to say that Marin did teach me about intimacy other than sex. She educated me about relationships. She taught me about how to be in a relationship. I'm lucky to have had that.

There were good and bad parts to our marriage. All those things that were good in our marriage are why we're still friends today. We're very in tune in how we see the world. There were differences between us too. For example, Marin doesn't like to go out. I like to go out and be part of a crowd, whereas she'd rather go to a small intimate setting and have some wine with friends. I like variation. So, yeah—I like going to a small quiet restaurant tonight, and then next week, let's do something different.

I think where we had conflict was that we were both alpha personalities. For the sake of the relationship, I think I acquiesced frequently. I gave in. To me, that's the way things are supposed to be. That's part of what a relationship is. When I said that Marin educated me about how to be in a relationship, I also mean that I learned the things that were missing from our relationship that I would like to see in a new relationship.

I haven't been completely successful at it. It's a matter of being able to sit down, understand that we're going to have conflict, that we're going to express how we feel about it, and that there's going to be an emotional response. Are you willing to accept the emotional response? That's really what defines the relationship and what defines it as a positive relationship. It's not that you can't be angry or that you're never going to be mad. It's that I understand you're angry about something, but I can expect at some point in the future you're going to get over it and move on, as opposed to using it as a weapon.

Marin and I evolved through that process. I'll give an example. Before we were married, there was a social dance she wanted to go to, and I didn't want to go. Marin held it against me for years. Eventually it got to the point where she was going to have to let that go, or it was going to affect our relationship if she didn't. When you're in that place where it does affect the relationship, it's time to do something about the relationship.

We didn't have kids. I think we probably would still be married if we'd had children. Marin asked me to leave because she wasn't happy. She believes that some of that has to do with sexuality, and that's how she justifies it. I don't agree, but there's no reason to argue that point. I believe that our differences existed outside of sexuality. We're both very strong personalities. I have my opinions, I have my beliefs, and I'm resolved to stand by them. That's where she and I had conflicts.

We've been separated for four years. Time has moved forward, and I've been able to let go of and forget about the bad things that occurred in our relationship. Otherwise, it would have been a positive when she asked me to leave. That would have allowed me to go and open up to my sexuality and pursue a different relationship.

It's not just about me being gay. I believe it also has to do with age and opportunity. I have single friends who are over forty, and—straight or gay—they have trouble finding a relationship that they're happy with. I think there are people who've been in relationships because it's reminiscent of the movie—this is "as good as it gets." They believe it won't get any better and they're not going to find anyone better.

I have a friend who's dated a number of different guys and hasn't found a relationship that he wants to make long term. I think the only difference between the gay world and the straight is that time occurs at a different speed in each. Everything is time-compressed in the gay world. I don't think it's a joke when people say that a lesbian's second date is a U-Haul, and a second date for gay men is ... What second date? Lesbians in general move faster in relationships than either gay men or straight people do.

But even for gay men, things are compressed. In the straight world, there are books, magazine articles, and other outlets of mainstream culture that promote what a proper relationship looks like. There is nothing like that in the gay world. Girls are taught that, to be proper, they need to put off having sex until there's at least an emotional bond. A lot of times sex comes too early, and that probably helps produce failures and divorces in straight and gay relationships. With gay men, sex generally happens right at the start of the relationship before there is any emotional bonding.

In my relationship with Marin, the sex waned. That was her choice, not mine. But there were enough positives in the relationship that allowed us to stay married for fifteen years. But as I said before, I think that having kids would have allowed us to stay married, even if things between us weren't working perfectly anymore.

Did I ever cheat on my wife? I never had sex with another woman while I was married. I mentioned earlier that I'd had one sexual encounter with a man several years before I got married and then I put that part of my life on a shelf. When I was in my mid-thirties, I took it off the shelf. I was traveling for business a lot, and I started experimenting. That's where

I guess I got my sex fix. At one point in time, I was out of town every week and, for a year and a half, I was going to the same city every month. So I was able to see the same people over and over.

I guess I'm a serial monogamist. I didn't have a guy in every port. I was more inclined to have a relationship develop. You know—let's talk, let's hang out, let's do things together. The level of hanging out was limited because I had to work until five or six o'clock every day and I had to get up early. So it wasn't like there were huge chunks of time that we could spend together.

Marin didn't know about this. It's something she doesn't know about and my family doesn't know about. The guys I was with, they knew that I was married. I told them that right from the start. And I did develop a relationship—a bond—with some of them. Some I still communicate with today.

—Separation—

Marin and I had a very amicable separation and divorce. I think that we're better apart than we were together. She knows now that I'm gay. She's met my partner.

I talk to Marin on a daily basis. We even socialize together. She and her boyfriend have been to our place. We socialize as couples. We maintain a very good relationship just not between the two of us but including our partners as well.

Her boyfriend seems to be better equipped at dealing with this than my boyfriend does. I think that Marin's boyfriend has other stuff going on that distracts him from the insecurities others would feel. He was married and divorced and has kids. I think that I'm the least of his concerns. Whereas the guy that I've been dating for four years, his name is Tom, he feels there's a competition going on—which there isn't. I think the part that confuses him is that I'm still in a relationship with my ex-wife. That's unusual in a straight relationship, and it's even more unusual in a gay relationship.

I still have very strong ties with my in-laws. Marin says that they processed all this, and they decided that I'm just their son. I still go to all their family functions.

One thing Marin would acknowledge is that she'd have a problem if I started to date other women. I think it helps her believe that the problem with our relationship was that I was gay.

—Ben's Life Now—

It would take us hours to talk about the dysfunction in my relationship with Tom. I should be better at relationships, but I'm not. Once again, I'm learning from the relationship that I'm in. I know I'll be much better in each relationship I go through. That's part of the learning curve.

I've been asked if I see myself as a gay man now or a bisexual. I haven't had a relationship with a woman since Marin so I assume I'm gay. In my experience, a lot of gay men are really negative toward bisexuals. I don't understand that. Their attitude is that either you're gay or you're straight. If you're bisexual, then you're messed up in the head, and we don't want to talk to you.

A better question to ask is, Do I think it would be easier to have a relationship with a woman at this point in time? I absolutely do. I think women are better wired to be in relationship. I think if you put two guys together, they know how to be guys together, not partners and lovers.

This is some of the conflict I have with Tom. He's a guy, but he wants to be treated like a woman. Not that this happens, but I'll use opening the door for him as an example. He'd like me to open the door for him, but he tells me that I don't have to do it. But he'd like it. But don't do it. There's a conflict in his own mind about it. And then, who opens the door for whom? There are gender roles that are played out in any relationship. Well, what happens when there's no clear gender role?

Here's another example. I tell him that I'll meet him someplace and he says, "Will you pick me up?" I tell him no. I never pick up my guy friends.

He says that I wouldn't do that to a woman. I treat him like a man, and he has a problem with that. Marin has helped me through that to some extent. I still don't understand it. He wants to be treated like a woman in some parts of the relationship—and I'm not talking about sex in any part of this.

It's about who plays what roles. It causes conflict in a relationship when you change that role and you're older. I mean, maybe if you're younger, you can evolve and get a better understanding of when that role switches in a gay relationship. I don't know. I don't have an answer. I think that's part of what it takes to be in a relationship.

I sometimes wonder what my life would be like if I had come out at age twenty rather than in my forties. Who I am has been shaped by twenty-plus years of living as an adult in the straight world. At thirty-five, I would go out to gay bars just to sit and watch the interactions and try to figure out if this was the life I wanted to live. Is that who I want to be? I did that for ten years—observed and collected information and thought, Is what I'm seeing enough to pull me toward this world?

If Marin hadn't asked me to leave, would I still be doing that? I don't know. I think we were mutually reaching a boiling point. I'm a person who's probably willing to take more than most. I probably should have made that choice and left my marriage ten years earlier. When she asked me to move out, I was numb for a long time. I went through a lot of therapy to get here.

I was sitting on my back porch one day looking at the sky, and in a brief moment I realized that I'm going to be okay. Of course, that realization went away, but then each day moved forward and as time progressed, things got better. The best analogy I can use is a scene from the movie *Sleepless in Seattle*. It's one of my favorite scenes in the movie. Tom Hanks is talking on the phone to the radio-show doctor. She asks him what his days are like. He says that he gets up and puts one foot on the floor and he keeps doing that day after day. When I heard that, I realized that I had a pretty amazing life, and I needed to keep moving forward each day. Nobody knows whether it's going to get better or not, but each day you move forward. You have to keep pushing yourself forward, or you get stuck.

—Advice—

What Should You Do?

If there's a doubt about whether you're gay or not, go for it. Go and experiment and find out if this is really what you want, away from any place where someone would judge you. For example, if you're not certain about it, then go to Rehoboth Beach, Delaware, or to a gay bar in a town you're visiting. Go and try it because the odds are that you're gay. The odds are that you're just trying to come to terms with it.

I would try to explore that part of myself and be secure. I'd explore that part of myself to the point where, if and when I was comfortable enough, I'd be able to just be gay—not a 'gay man,' but a man who is gay.

I spent ten years married to Marin and going to gay bars, observing and not participating in life, trying to figure out if this was the life I wanted to live. If you're in that position, take the leap and make a choice. Don't live life watching from the sidelines. As hard as you think it's going to be, it is— but it does get better.

Chapter 8

Grace

Grace is a forty-three-year-old teacher who was married twice: to Dan in 1994 and Luke in 2002. She and Luke are now separated, and they have a ten-year-old son. Grace has been attracted to women all her life, but she never really questioned it, because, as she said, "Of course, I was straight. Everybody was straight." Then she met Christine, a lesbian with whom she became friends. Even after it became apparent to Grace that she was deeply attracted to Christine, it took her about eighteen months to sort things out, which included talking with Luke about her feelings for Christine. The couple separated after Luke made it clear that it was okay with him for Grace to explore her feelings for Christine. Grace was in a relationship with Christine for two and a half years. She now lives with her son, maintains a close friendship with Luke, and is in a relationship with a man.

—Grace's Story—

I don't know that I ever questioned whether I was heterosexual or homosexual. I was raised Methodist, and I never thought about it too often. It just wasn't a conversation I had with myself. Looking back now, it's funny—because I've been attracted to women all my life, but I didn't see that in the same light as I do now.

It's not that I didn't notice that I was attracted to women. I don't think I called it that. I didn't sense that it was any different than just liking someone a lot. I didn't even know anyone could be gay, and so I saw it more as admiration than attraction. And I never really questioned it—because, of course, I was straight. Everybody was straight.

I was probably in high school before I had a coherent thought about what the word *gay* actually meant, and by then I was so conditioned that I didn't think to consider it in terms of my own self. Now I can see that I always checked out women. I'm attracted to women. I'm attracted to men too, but it's more like one in a hundred men versus one in five women. It's very different. But even as recently as ten years ago, I just wasn't conscious about it.

I'm still not submersed in gay culture in my daily life. I've dabbled around with it, but I'm living my life. I'm not out playing, or out in bars, or in a scene, or with a group of people who have an idea about how this is supposed to go. That's not me. I'm not that person. I'm raising my kid. I'm starting a business. I'm working.

—Marriage—

I've been married twice—the first time I was twenty-four, and the second time I was thirty-two. My first marriage—to Dan—didn't last very long. I think we were married three years all told, but we weren't together after about the first seven months. It was quick. My second husband was Luke, and he and I were together for twelve years. We weren't married for twelve years, but we were a couple for that long.

Was I in love with Dan when I married him? Ah, geez, I don't know. What does that really mean? Was I in reality and in love with him at the same time? No, I wasn't.

I don't mean to sound callous because of course I cared for him, but it goes back to my upbringing. I was having sex with Dan and was afraid my traditionally minded grandparents could suspect it. I loved and respected them, and couldn't bear the possibility of their disapproval, so when Dan proposed, I convinced myself I was supposed to marry him. At the time, I wasn't aware of anything I was creating. I was trying to do what I thought would please everybody else. I didn't think to question who I was or what I wanted.

Dan and I got married, and about thirty seconds later those questions I hadn't asked became extremely loud. *What did I just do?* Before the wedding, I did have a sense I wanted to call it off, but I didn't have the nerve. I convinced myself I had normal pre-wedding jitters and would be okay once the planning hype simmered down. At that time, I simply didn't see what I see now. I was a totally different person—completely inauthentic.

Once I went through with the wedding, it was like a veil lifted. I knew I'd made a serious mistake, and my life became all about survival for a time. It took a lot of courage, but it also was liberating for me to admit the errors in my judgment and to learn to be honest and stand on my own. I definitely learned a lot about who I was and the person I would become.

With Luke, it was different. I loved hanging out with Luke. For ten years, I lived with him and his children. He raised his kids after his wife left and moved to Florida. I loved him when we met, but he was less interested in me at the time. I was much younger than him. There were a lot of intense highs and lows between us over those ten years. The pendulum swung far in both directions, and the relationship was exhilarating and ultimately exhausting. We were finally about to end it when I got pregnant.

It was an interesting twist because, in all those years, we'd tried and given up on the idea of having a baby. Then all of sudden I was pregnant. So we got married. That really wasn't my first choice, but we talked about it and came to agree that it was best for the baby. Our arrangement was then and is still diplomatic and business-like.

One Tuesday afternoon after work, Luke and I met my mother at a small-town JP and got married. Afterward, I went grocery shopping. So when you ask me if I was in love with Luke—yeah, I loved Luke and I love his kids. I always have, and there was surely a time when I was in love with him. But when we got married, was it about our love for each other? No, definitely not—it was totally because we were trying to do the right thing.

Overall, it was a tumultuous relationship. It had uniquely fine strong points and some really awful weak points. Most of it was extreme that way. When our son Sam was born, I think I just gave up the fight. Whatever had us aggravating each other, I just didn't care about it anymore. I had this beautiful child, and he trumped everything.

Although my relationship with Luke had mostly been unhealthy, things got obviously easier between us after Sam was born, and I let go of a bunch of upset. Things loosened up, and I became free to talk to Luke about things that were important, and our relationship started to take a different turn. It shifted and became more of a friendship—a valuable alliance. Then I fell in love with someone else.

—Christine—

I met Christine while I was married to Luke, and it was immediately clear to me that I was attracted to her. I knew that she was gay, but I didn't necessarily think it was something I needed to deal with. Yet the more time I spent with her, the more clear I was that I wanted to be with her, and what I felt wasn't just admiration.

We didn't have an affair. We had a friendship at the onset. I had a conversation with another friend about my feelings for Christine, and my friend was very compassionate about my experience of being between a rock and a hard place. I had an overwhelming desire to explore my feelings for Christine, but I also desperately needed to maintain my integrity in my marriage to Luke. She finally suggested that I talk to Luke. "Are you kidding me?" I said. That was the last thing I wanted to do. That sounded completely crazy. My friend said, "Well, consider that he already knows." I thought about it for a long time and then concluded it was actually my best option. So eventually I did talk openly and honestly with him.

Luke already knew that Christine and I were friends, but he didn't know about my feelings for her. When I told him, he said, "Ah, well, that's what's been going on with you. I had no idea what it was, but I knew it was something." So we began the process of working through an ordeal. Luke became a source of comfort, helping me sort through my self-judgment and confusion. Here I had finally just settled down. Our son was just about three years old. I really felt selfish and kind of crazy. I'm still very grateful that Luke was so accepting and reassuring and such a good friend to me.

Christine and I didn't get together right away. It took about a year and a half for me to sort things out. During that time, Luke and I continued to talk a lot. We said everything there was to say. If anything didn't work for either of us, we'd stop and look at it until gradually a path became clear to us both that would suit and respect everyone involved. Then we made an action plan and executed it.

I moved out with an agreement that Luke and I would always honor each other and be the best friends and best parents we could be. We promised each other to have the best separation possible, and to keep truing ourselves up to our agreement, again and again.

After Luke and I separated, Christine and I stayed together for two and a half years. My relationship with Christine has been the most significant relationship in my life. I really thought she was the one, but unfortunately things didn't work out the way I thought they would.

Christine and I never lived together. We both wanted to, but when we got together, I had just moved out of the house I'd shared with Luke. I think that maybe she wanted to move the relationship along faster than I felt I could go at the time. She was in more of a hurry, and she needed to solidify and cement and validate our partnership in a way that felt inauthentic to me. I didn't feel the need to create a lot of structure and convention around our relationship. I just wanted to love her and let things evolve naturally in their own sweet time.

It was very sweet, the time I spent with Christine. I think ultimately we wanted the same things. I just didn't want it all immediately. We didn't find a way to accept and see each other through our personal differences.

I was newly separated with a young child. I had a demanding job, and there were other important things happening in my life at the time, including my dad getting sick and dying. I finally felt at home in my own skin, and just wanted to relax and bask in the glory. I just couldn't move into the stress of plans and moves and time frames and hustle bustle and more big life changes. Somehow I failed to communicate all that in a way that left Christine feeling secure about my love and commitment. Things just didn't work out, and we ended it in frustration.

About a year later, I started hanging out with an old friend who was having his own share of heartache, and as we comforted each other, we became lovers. After some time, Christine came back into my life, and we tried again. My male friend had no issue with my relationship with Christine, but wanted to remain close and befriend her as well. She was not open to a relationship with him. She had concerns about our romantic involvement, and asked me to choose between them. I wasn't willing to lose or risk hurting either of them, so I took no action. Christine ended our relationship via text: "Don't call me. Don't text me. Don't email me. I do not wish to have any further communication with you."

I've reached out to her since then, hoping for forgiveness and a fresh start. It was after something important happened in my son's life and also after I learned she'd had a bad car accident. Christine hasn't responded. I still think about her every day. I've made peace with my sorrow by accepting that I may always love her but may never express it again in a physical relationship with her. It's almost like she's dead—only I know she's alive and choosing not to be with me. That's difficult to bear.

—Coming Out—

During the eighteen months when I was with Luke and talking with him about my feelings for Christine, I learned how important it was for me to talk to the people whose lives would be affected by this relationship. When I started talking with Luke about this, I wasn't even sure I was going to do anything about my attraction to Christine, but I knew that I needed to talk with him.

My head was definitely not in the game with him anymore. I had already checked out. I just wasn't talking with him about what was happening inside me. So communicating with him about what was going on for me about Christine cleared up a lot between us. I felt like I was going crazy, and he assured me that I wasn't crazy. He actually became an ally for me. It was weird. It didn't go the way I would have predicted. And the only reason I ended up having a straight conversation with him was because a friend told me to.

I know a lot of people are afraid to have that kind of conversation with their partner because what they share could be used against them. I think that's especially true for people who have kids.

Once I started to sort through my feelings for Christine and to talk with Luke, the possibility of being with her started to become more real. I knew that she was going to be part of my life, so I had to let people know what the deal was. There were only three people I needed to tell immediately: my sister, my dad, and my mom. That's in addition to Luke and Sam, of course, but I was already talking with them.

My sister was just loving and very supportive. She was kind of like, "Well, of course you're gay." When she said that, it was like, "Okay, now I can just relax into this instead of resisting it."

I don't remember exactly what my dad said, but I was most fearful of his reaction. The hardest part was spilling my words out loud. Turns out, he was already distracted by something my sister had just told him, and he made a joke about how she and I were running interference for each other. That was perfect. In the end, he was welcoming and very nice to Christine.

His wife—my stepmother—had more of an issue with it. She kept telling me not to talk with people about my relationship with Christine. I think that both she and my dad were probably afraid I'd lose my job because I was with Christine. But they were also open and loving because they wanted me to be happy. And although they did love Christine, my dad also made it clear to me that public displays of affection were not going to be tolerated. I felt very little freedom to express my love for her in front of them—not that they would have said anything to embarrass me in the moment, but it would have upset them.

Then there was my mom. She was more difficult than I expected. She said all the right things—like "It's your choice" and "I'll love you no matter what" and "I just want you to be happy." But then she would express another side of how she felt—things like "What did I do wrong?" and "I have to hide this." She felt that she had to hide my relationship with Christine from her side of the family. She didn't want her relatives to know.

I'm very close with my grandmother, and I'm pretty much of a straight shooter anyway. I had a hard time not saying anything to her. I didn't like that. I felt like I was lying. It ended up that my uncle's wife figured it out herself, and let me know I was safe with her. She and I have had a deep connection since I was a young girl. She'd met Christine, seen us together, and she's not stupid. I like to think my grandmother figured it out too, but I kept quiet.

Christine came to all our family functions. It was clear that she was my partner, but then my mom was acting like we weren't really partners. That went on for a long time. I finally told my grandmother about my love for Christine, which she accepted in the blink of an eye. By that time, Christine and I had already broken up, and she hadn't been around my family in a while. My grandmother asked, "Well, if you love her, why aren't you with her?"

My mom and I … I'm still hesitant with her. I can't ask for much more really. I just wish that I didn't make her ashamed. I sense that. She'd never say that, but I've felt like she was ashamed and didn't want people to know.

My family's been very supportive of my life choices overall, but no one supports me in having a future with Christine anymore. It ended badly for me, and no one wants to see me in pain. There's some beautiful bit of my self-expression that was completely unleashed in my relationship with Christine, but there's no space for it anymore. In reality, she's no longer part of my life.

—Grace's Life Now—

Although our marriage didn't work out, my relationship with Luke has transformed and actually works much better now. We're able to work together, be friends, and spend generous time with Sam, both individually and as a family. We're very close.

When Luke and I parted, that was probably the best, most empowering experience I've ever had in a relationship. It was really clean. That doesn't mean that it all goes smoothly all the time. Every now and then, something happens and one of us temporarily loses out, but we steer things right back on track and honor our commitment to being the best we can be for our son, for each other, and for our families. Legally, for tax and insurance purposes, Luke and I are still married.

If I had it to do over again, would I marry Dan and Luke? I don't know. I hedge. I've learned a tremendous amount about myself through these two "failures." I would not be who I am today without those experiences, and I'm pretty happy with how I've turned out so far. Also, what's smack in the middle of my marriage with Luke is our son Sam, and having him is definitely the best thing I've ever done.

Sam doesn't want us to be divorced. He's aware that we're not in love, that we have other partners, and don't want to live together. For him, none of that is bad, but if you put the word *divorce* in the mix, immediately he's panic stricken. I'm not sure what that's about. When he's a little older and more emotionally mature, we'll see if he thinks differently about it. But for now, it's working fine for us the way it is.

Also, for the past two years, I've been in a light-hearted relationship with my male friend. It's not too serious, which is perfect, and I'm grateful for his patience and easy-going way. There's a lot he could be uptight about. My situation is messy, and I'm open and honest about all of it. I'm married, I have a son, I'm in love with someone I can't be with, but I'm still open to being in a relationship. Anyone who enters into a relationship with me has to be able to accept all that, as confounding as it may seem.

If I had it to do all over again, I don't know if I'd choose to be in a relationship with a woman rather than a man. Maybe, maybe not. It doesn't mean that much to me whether I'm gay or straight. That doesn't seem to define me—so I don't really care if I'm gay or straight.

What I'm not sure about is marriage. I almost wonder if I'm staying married to Luke to make sure that I don't marry anybody else. It keeps me safe. I guess I'd like to find my way back there. I don't have the best track record or role models to give me inspiration. I'd love to have a committed, monogamous relationship with a partner who I could share my love, happiness, and time with. In my thinking, the recognition of union by the state is irrelevant to the foundation of a relationship, except in terms of business and finance (including health care). Marriage is practical, but in my experience it is not sacred. I suppose I'm still looking for what is sacred in a relationship.

I came close to that in my relationship with Christine. For me, being with her was very different from being in a relationship with a man. That might seem obvious to some people, but I was surprised that it was so different. The things I had to work on to sustain that relationship were nothing like I'd experienced with men.

It was more difficult for me to be in a relationship with a woman, and when I say that, I'm looking at how it went. My relationship with Christine didn't go the way I wanted it to go, so of course it was—in my opinion—more difficult for me. I probably would prefer to be with a woman even though it's far easier for me to be with a man. With a man, I don't have to deal with the safety of public displays of affection. If I want to give him a kiss or hold his hand or touch him in public, I don't have to worry about whether it's safe to do that. There's no stigma attached to a man and a woman showing affection in public.

The other thing is that guys seem to me to be much more easygoing in general. Things don't bug them so much, like if my house is perfect or not. I'm just using that as an example. Men seem easier to please because they don't have as much attention on small imperfections. And that's fine. Their attention seems to be somewhere else, and I feel less pressure to be perfect.

Before my relationship with Christine, I always wanted to be the center of a man's attention. Since I've been with Christine, I'm far less concerned with that. Guys—they don't seem to mind much what I'm up to. It just doesn't concern them. *Oh, you're going somewhere, and I won't see you for a while. Okay. Bye.* Men's easy acceptance, the way they just roll with things, used to make me feel like they don't care, but it's not an issue for me anymore. I don't exactly know why. I think I saw my suspicious, uptight self reflected back to me in my relationship with Christine, and I didn't like how that way of being left me feeling. Not that Christine actually was like me, but I saw myself clearly in her, and I realized I'd rejected a lot of love over the course of my life due to my own absurd fear of the unknown. And those experiences hadn't left me feeling very good about myself.

That was a good learning experience, although I haven't figured out how to transfer it back into a relationship with a woman. I haven't really had much of an opportunity either. Part of me is … my heart is still in the past with Christine.

I should point out that my heart was in that relationship with Christine unlike it's been in any other. With her, I felt like I could love and give my whole heart. I felt more known and present with Christine, more alive and real. I felt more at home in my own skin. I felt more like I knew who I was and what I was about. I felt safe to feel deeply and express my love openly, even if it seemed schmaltzy, and even during sex. I feel thwarted in this level of expression with a man. This part of me has never felt safe or nurtured in my relationships with men.

These are totally unrealistic expectations for me to place on my male partner. I've tried to communicate my experience and desire, to recreate it, and he's really not sure what I'm talking about.

Where this disconnect really shows up is in the area of sex, which was very tender with Christine. Our connection was very strong. There were female sensibilities. There was conversation around sex. There were more dimensions to sex, and we were really present. It hasn't been that way for me with men. After hiding my softness for so many years, it was such a revelation that Christine wanted my sweet side to see the light of day. *Oh, my God. No, no. Let's have that sweet side.* It was really scary at first to let go and just be me, but then it was, oh, so good.

Of course, now I want to be able to express that. There's a place there that was my place. I now value my own sweetness too, because I know that it's possible for it to exist in the world without getting trampled. But I still don't feel my true self is appropriate sexually with men. I still feel that I have to stand guard and shroud my tenderness. Perhaps that's why sex is not a feature of my current relationship.

—Advice—

Talk with Your Spouse

I have a friend who used to do a one-man show. He would read his poetry and perform monologues and songs. One of his pieces was about a man who was married and didn't tell his wife he was having sex with another man. That was twenty years ago, but I still remember being horrified by that story.

I would hate to have a partner lie to me that way. I find it extremely disturbing. On one level, there's the betrayal of being married to someone who's cheating and lying, as well as potentially exposing you to sexually transmitted diseases you don't know to protect yourself against because you think you're in a monogamous relationship. On another level, you're shut out of your partner's true feelings and desires, and you have no chance to ever contribute to your partner being fulfilled.

I believe that in certain cultures and communities, the phenomenon of having a secret sex life is more prevalent. Men are married to women and have sex with other men. Maybe that allows them to believe that they're not gay.

My advice would be to handle things responsibly with your spouse, and be true to yourself, and be in communication with your spouse before you jump into another relationship. Don't let it get to the point where you're acting out and not dealing with what you're doing. Keep everything in service to the relationship you're currently in. I mean, you can't sit down and tell your husband or wife that you think you're gay without things getting messy. The chances are good that it's going to be messy and people may be upset.

I think it's more difficult to talk with your spouse if you've already had sex with someone else. Once that's happened—once you've cheated—it's a lot harder for your spouse to be generous in their ability to listen to you and talk with you. If I had had sex with Christine and then came back to talk with Luke, it would not have gone as well. There would have been all this hurt and betrayal to overcome before we could have the important conversation. It would have been a hellacious mess. Some people may think my situation is a hellacious mess anyhow, but I think I'm blessed.

It's essential to communicate to people you trust who are stakeholders before you do anything. That can help sort things out too, because otherwise you just have these crazy ideas spinning around inside your head. It can help to get other points of view and feedback.

I think if you've not done anything yet that's outside the boundaries of your marriage—if you're just communicating about what you're thinking and feeling—it's a lot more likely to bring you and your spouse closer, whether the two of you stay together or not. My conversations with Luke definitely made us way closer. They put a whole new realm of reality and authenticity into our relationship that wasn't there before.

It isn't like the conversation I had with Luke was immediately all about joy. There were definitely lots of things that came up that we had to talk about to get through it, but we kept tackling it. We kept communication open—and, yeah, there were times when I didn't want to communicate because it was like my private little secret that I didn't want to share with anybody. I didn't want it to see the light of day. I was afraid of what somebody might try to do to it.

But if I hadn't been in communication with Luke, I never would have acted on my desire to be with Christine. Even though it didn't work out with her, it was one of the more beautiful experiences that I've ever had. I don't regret it at all.

Part 2

Issues to Consider:

Things to Be Aware of
If You're in a Straight Marriage and
Questioning If You Are Gay

Chapter 9
What About the Kids?

"Eve and Stephanie and I would sometimes talk about women loving women and men loving men. One time, Eve said, 'Mom, why are people mad about that? When you love somebody, that's really good.' The wisdom of a child ..."
—Erin, speaking about her daughters

Six of the eight people I interviewed for this book have children. All of us were concerned about how our coming out would affect our children. Several of us were afraid that we might lose custody.

The fears and challenges that gay parents face are not all that different from those of straight parents going through a divorce. You don't have to be gay to worry that something you do might harm or burden your children, or that your ex might try to restrict your ability to be with them, or that it might be challenging to find a new partner who will accept your children and co-parent them with you. None of those concerns are limited to gay parents. For people who are in a straight marriage and considering coming out as gay, however, fears about how their coming out will impact their children—and their relationship with their children—can be daunting. Those fears can make it even harder to know what to do.

Here are some of our stories about coming out to our children and how coming out affected our relationships with our children.

—Adam—

Adam told his three children that he was gay as part of the same conversation in which he and his wife told them they were separating. He explained that it was difficult to decide what to tell them when. "Kate and I really battled with that," he said. "There were some people who said that's a lot for the kids to take in at one time. To be honest, nobody said that we should talk with them about all of it at one time. But what all those people didn't realize was what a strong family we are. There was no way we could have told our kids that we were separating without telling them why. It would have been too big a disconnect otherwise."

Adam explained that all their lives, his children had watched Kate and him cook, laugh, smile, and dance together in the house. "They were always telling us to quit kissing—that we were making them sick. They'd never seen us fight—and remember, the youngest was in his late teens at the time we separated. All they'd ever seen was a loving relationship. If we didn't tell them why we were separating—if I didn't tell them I was gay—they would have inevitably started making up things, like thinking that one of us was having an affair. We felt that we owed them the truth. I didn't want them to have to try to figure out what could have possibly gone wrong."

If Kate and he had had a contentious, unloving relationship with a lot of fighting, he said, then there would have been no need for an explanation. "We would have told them that we were getting divorced, and they probably would have thought, *It's about time. You two don't get along. Thank God you're getting a divorce.* That wasn't the case. With us, it was the complete opposite. And they reacted like someone had died. It was that traumatic for them … until I told them why."

It's been years now since Adam and Kate separated, and he said that his kids are all doing well with his coming out, although his older daughter still struggles a bit with it. "She's religious and her husband is a pastor," he explained. "I think she struggles a bit because she knows there's nothing wrong with me, and she knows I'm not a bad person, but I think it's a struggle for her to make sense of it all. But she's very supportive and loving toward me and so is her husband."

Adam said that his relationship with his children is still basically the same except for one thing. "Sometimes I feel a little on the outside of things," he said. "When they come to town, they always stay with their mom. She lives in the house they grew up in, and it's comfortable and familiar to them.

I understand it, and I'm fine with it. It's just that sometimes I feel a little like I'm on the outside looking in."

He noted that his children have made only one request of him regarding dating: "They've asked me not to drag a lot of people in and out of their lives, to wait till I feel comfortable that this is somebody I want to be with before introducing them to my kids. I can respect that. That's good advice for anybody who has children and is dating."

—Drew—

For Drew, parting from Susan was almost as difficult as living with her. They went through a contentious divorce and then a contentious custody battle. Susan sought sole custody of their two children. Drew sought shared custody. He got the best attorney he could afford.

This is how he described the custody hearing and its aftermath: "During the custody hearing, Susan's attorneys tried to bring up the fact that I'm gay, as though I was some lesser human being because I was gay. The judge swung around in his chair, looked at my ex-wife and her counsel, and abruptly declared, 'That is completely irrelevant!' He later handed down his decision in my favor. It was a glorious day for my kids and me. Gay or straight, being a good parent is a choice and something that you need to make a priority. Being gay does not make you a bad parent."

Drew noted that the irony of his story is that as his children have gotten older, they've wanted to spend more and more of their time with him. At the time of our interview, they were living with Drew practically full time. "My ex-wife, who wanted to deny me any time with my children, now has children who don't want to be with her," he laughed quietly and shook his head. "There is karma."

Drew has never had a specific conversation with his son and daughter to tell them he is gay. "My kids were so young when I came out," he explained. "Gay is how they know me. It's natural for them that I have relationships with men. As far as they're concerned, life is just that way. Whenever I've been in a relationship with a man, my kids have never made it an issue, and neither have their friends or the parents of their friends. It's just what's so." He added that he and his son, who is now in his late teens, recently had a conversation in which his son said that he just wants Drew to be happy. "He said he hopes I meet someone who'll be good to me."

—Trudy—

Asked if her sons know that she's a lesbian, Trudy answered, "Absolutely."

How did she tell them? Did she have a specific conversation with them? She said that she did but explained that she was careful about when she had that conversation with them.

"They knew that I had good women friends and that our house was always full of women," she said. "We'd have dinners all the time with lots of women there. I'm trying to think how old they were when I actually used the word *lesbian*. I mean, they knew who I was. By the time they were teenagers, I think they'd figured it out. If they had asked me, I'd have told them, but I didn't want to give them a word that they couldn't use in a way that wouldn't cause them trouble. The word *lesbian* seemed very loaded to me for them. They were in their teens when I talked with them. I just told them that I liked women and I hoped they understood that and would respect me as they always had. And they were like, 'Yeah. Cool, mom. No big deal.' They knew it. It was that easy."

Trudy then told me the following story as an example of how comfortable her sons seem to be with her being a lesbian. A year ago, in honor of her retirement, she was named the grand marshal of the Pride Parade in Pittsburgh. She was riding down the street in a convertible, and one of her sons and some of his friends were standing on a street corner. She heard her son yell out, "Mom, I love you." She explained, "That was really nice. There I was, the grand marshal of this Gay Pride Parade, and he wasn't embarrassed to yell out that he loves me in front of his friends."

—Gene—

Gene's daughter Bennett was seventeen—a junior in high school—when he and I spoke.

"When she was five," Gene said, "I had to sit her down on my lap to tell her I was leaving. It was the hardest thing I've ever had to do." Most parents who've had to explain a separation or divorce to their children can empathize with Gene about how difficult that conversation can be.

But compared to many divorced fathers, Gene's experience since that conversation has been easy. "I've never had a rigid schedule with Casey regarding our daughter," he explained. "Whatever works is what we do. We've never fought over who got to spend time with Bennett when. That's not even an issue with us. If I'm home and I call Bennett and she wants to stay with me for the weekend, that's fine. If she wants to stay with her mom, that's fine too. Now that she's getting older, I see less of her, and that's harder for me—but I think that's true for many parents of teenagers."

When Gene talks about Bennett, he describes her as being "just wonderful" and "the perfect daughter." He was dismayed to learn recently that his daughter had been dealing with issues that he had no idea existed. "Even when I was living at home," he said, "I traveled a lot for work, and I was away a lot. Bennett would get angry, and she used to take her anger out on my wife. It took some time for me to figure out that she was angry with me. Because I was home so little, she didn't want me to see that anger so she would always take it out on Casey. Now that's changed. I just texted my ex-wife, saying that Bennett seems to be angry with me or to resent me. Clearly there's something going on. I know she's stressed out. She's coming to the end of school with her finals."

Gene said that he suspects that Bennett is coming to terms with his being gay. "She just started therapy a couple weeks ago. It was so tough getting her there but now she loves this therapist, so I'm hoping she's working out her issues. I would love to go too, to help her out. There's that big gay white elephant in the room that's never been discussed."

Although he has never had a specific conversation with Bennett telling her that he is gay, Gene said that his daughter knows that he is a gay man—without question. She knows that Jake is his partner. He and Jake use the term "my partner" when they refer to one another. He recently started writing a letter to her to try to explain this all to her.

He said, "You think they're well adjusted, but my ex-wife just told me something that I was completely unaware of. She said, 'Do you realize that Bennett went all these years through school and made some friends but never had any close friends that she could really tell about her life?' She could never open up to me about what kind of life she's had. That's tough for her but it's also tough for me knowing how difficult it's been for her."

Gene explained that he does try to talk to his daughter. "I try," he said. "Bennett's now learning through her therapist that she's better off telling me things, because it hurts me more when she doesn't tell me something than when she does. Bennett's always been afraid of my reaction, which I don't understand, but it makes sense to her."

Since he's learned of the issues that Bennett is having, Gene said that he has tried to be more sensitive to her. He told the following story as an example. "The other day, I was checking my nieces' and nephews' Facebook pages, and I noticed something I hadn't been aware of before. They all taunt their friends by writing things like 'Oh, you're such a fag' and 'You're so gay' and 'You're a homo.' So I texted them to remind them that not only do they have an uncle who's gay, but they also have a cousin who could be sensitive to how people use the word *gay*. I suggested that they have a bit more compassion and stop saying those things. Actually it's never bothered me that people say things like that, but now that I have a daughter who could be bothered by it, I just want them to be aware of what they're saying."

—Erin—

Erin knew she was a lesbian when she was separated from her husband Jack, but she waited until her divorce was final before she became involved with another woman. "As a lesbian, you could lose your kids back then," she explained. "That wasn't an *if*. It was definite."

She didn't talk with many of her friends about being a lesbian for the same reason. She told me, "I didn't want to take the risk that Jack might take me to court and my friends might be called to testify. If that had happened, they would have been stuck having to choose between lying and feeling like they were betraying me. That's one way it was very different then from now. You can't lose your kids now on the basis of being a sexual minority. Back then you could lose your parental rights if you were gay or a prostitute. I knew that very clearly, and I hired an attorney who knew that I was out and knew to be careful." Once her divorce was final, Erin was able to come out to her ex-husband and her friends.

I asked how she came out to her daughters. She said that she did talk with them, but even before she had a specific conversation with them, Eve and Stephanie had grown up around gay culture. When Erin went to gay political events, she would sometimes take her daughters with her. She explained that the gay men loved her girls, and the girls loved all the attention they got.

"Eve and Stephanie grew up with homosexuality politically before they had to deal with it personally," Erin said. "They were among the few children who were around the gay community a lot. There was a gay coffee house, and one day I went there with my girls. Stephanie was about five, and she was invited to sing. She sang 'Kookaburra.' When she sang the line 'Gay your life must be,' she got a standing ovation."

Erin said that her daughters met a lot of people, and people were very open and honest with them. "So they knew," Erin explained. "I know we talked about my being a lesbian, but it was usually when one of them asked a question—particularly before my divorce was final."

She gave the following example of how casual her conversations with them were. "One day, we were in the car listening to NPR. A book on homosexuality had just come out, and Eve asked, 'Mom, what's homosexuality?' She must have been nine at the time. I said, 'That's when a man loves a man or a woman loves a woman.' And she said, 'Oh, like you and Karen.' I said yeah. And that was the end of it."

Erin used to work with children. "Kids are really good. Kids know," she explained. "When I was working with kids from gay or lesbian couples, they weren't ever mad that their parents were gay. They were angry when their parents didn't tell them they were gay—particularly since the kids usually knew anyway."

—Grace—

Grace's son Sam was nine years old at the time of our interview. He was four when Grace separated from her husband Luke and began a relationship with Christine.

"Christine and I were clearly a couple," Grace explained. "We didn't live together, but we were always together at her place or mine, and Sam was usually with us."

Asked if Sam ever had an issue with Grace being with a woman, this is how she responded: "It's interesting. I don't think Sam thought there was anything abnormal about two women being together when I was with Christine. But then he started school and began getting more information from outside our home about same-sex relationships. I remember he came home one day and said something about two boys being together. 'Oh, that's gross,' he said. I asked, 'Well, what about Christine and me? Is that gross too?' Then I brought up another couple we know, 'And what about Jill and Sue?' He didn't say anything—but I could see he made the connection, and it was something for him to think about."

After she and Christine broke up, Grace talked with Sam several times about the possibility of her being in a relationship with Christine again. He would say, "I don't have any problem with you being with her, as long as you can be happy." Grace explained that Sam is older now, and his problems with Christine are more vivid for him than their time together is. He remembers the breakup and how hard that was. She said that Christine was absent from their lives for a year and a half and wouldn't communicate, and then came back for six months only to leave again after more upset. Now it's been another long time with no communication—and Sam has had to deal with all that.

"Sam adored Christine," Grace explained. "When she and I were together, they were very close. We still talk about it sometimes, and I still feel sad. We had a lot of fun together, and the three of us were our own family. A while back I was bemoaning the fact that she left me, and he said, 'Well, get over it, Mom. She did leave you, and she left me too.' I hadn't really been aware that he saw it that way. Perhaps I just didn't want to see that."

Grace believes that Sam would prefer her to be with a man, because it would make their lives simpler, and they could talk about sports and other guy things. He's said as much. "But I also know that if I were with a woman," Grace added, "Sam would figure out a way to make that work and accept it too. He truly wants me to be happy. He's said that, too."

Chapter 10
Safety

*"I'm very close to a woman who is mixed race. I sometimes think
... that there are significant numbers of people who've never met her
but don't like her. That's what it's like to be gay.
There are thousands of men who would drag me behind a pickup truck
if they had the chance."*
—Adam

If you're looking at coming out, one of the issues that you need to consider is safety. It's an issue that can take several forms, including safety from violence (both physical and non-physical) and safety from sexually transmitted disease.

—Safety from Violence—

Let's face it. There are places in the world—even in the United States—where you put your safety in jeopardy by coming out. There are also families in which that's true. Although safety from violence will not be an issue for most people reading this book, it is a vital issue for those whose safety may be at risk.

Safety was one of the issues that Adam spoke about. "Any time you have to be careful about who you are, it's not good. I'm very close to a woman who is mixed race. I sometimes think how hard it has to be for her to know that there are significant numbers of people who've never met her but don't like her. That's what it's like to be gay. There are thousands of men who would drag me behind a pickup truck if they had the chance."

Safety was one of the issues I spoke about with Betty Hill, the Executive Director of Persad in Pittsburgh. Safety is a matter of degree, she said, rather than an either-or condition. "Sometimes I think about this idea of the closet door and I wonder, *How did people get in there?* They went into the closet or were put in there by the belief that it's safer to hide than to be who they are. We get a lot of messages—both subtle and overt—that being homosexual is not okay, and so it becomes a good thing to hide. It becomes safer to hide. So we hide because of perceived or real unsafety in the world."

Betty explained that people have varying degrees of safety around them depending on their situations. There are some families that are very open and welcoming to the person coming out, and others that are very negative and closed about homosexuality or believe that it's unacceptable. Family negativity sometimes has a religious basis. When that's the case, it is usually based on the belief that being gay is wrong, shameful, or sinful, and some families cannot get over that. There are also cultural groups—Latinos and African Americans to name two—that consider homosexuality inappropriate or unnatural, and that disapproval may also have religious roots.

When I interviewed her, Kathy spoke about her fear of being open about her sexuality with very religious people. "I'm open about my sexuality, except in some situations where I'm not. It seems like mostly where I'm not open is around people who are highly religious. I may be stereotyping them, but I find that people with strong religious beliefs—not spiritual, but religious beliefs—are very … I'm scared to tell them."

She said that she had worked at a company where her boss was very Christian. He read the bible every day. "There was no way that I felt I could ever come out at work and share anything about my sexuality," she explained. "That's an area that I would love to see come along to where people are more accepting. My brother was always accepting of me, and my parents were both deceased when I came out so I didn't have to deal with any family disapproval. The one area where I still feel there is the greatest homophobia is organized religion."

Just as there are some people to whom it is not safe to come out, whether that lack of safety is real or imagined, there are also locales where it may not be safe to be open about homosexuality. Another way to state that is there are places where it is better to be smart about whom you come out to.

In the U.S., there tends to be greater acceptance of homosexuality in urban environments than in some rural areas. That's my opinion. In some settings, open homosexuality is so uncommon that it's feared and thought of as an abomination. Even in these settings—in the most culturally rigid parts of the world and the most conservative religious families—homosexuality exists, and homosexual men and women find themselves in a situation where coming out can entail not only loss of family and community, but also a threat to their physical safety.

Betty and I spoke about what happens as a person begins to come out. Sometimes coming out is a process of self-realization. Sometimes it happens with the help of other people or by telling other people. She explained, "For some people, it becomes more unsafe to be in the closet than out, and that experience of not safety is usually more emotional pain than anything—depression, not being able to stand yourself, or the lack of authenticity from lying to people you care about. All those things can drive the need to come out, where it's more unsafe to be in the closet than it is to be out."

So what does someone who wants to come out of the closet do if they're in a family or environment in which it's not safe to come out? According to Betty, it's a matter of being aware of the risks and managing those risks. Organizations like Persad help people look at what's in the closet and what's outside, what their circumstances are, what choices they have, and how to prepare for the choices they make.

There are some risks one can prepare for. For example, one of the threats for a man who's married and has kids is losing his kids if he comes out. That threat is relatively easy to prepare for. He might need to meet with an attorney to get clear about his custody options and parental rights. In the United States, we have a general cultural bias toward giving custody of children to their mothers (but that is changing rapidly), so men today fear the loss of their children much more than women do. That's not to say that women don't have that fear as well. Many lesbians fear that their sexuality will be used as a reason to take away their parental rights, although for men it tends to be a bigger issue.

Other risks are more difficult to prepare for. I would think that most people recognize whether their physical safety might be in jeopardy if they come out. But being aware that you're in a potentially abusive environment is not the same thing as being able to avoid abuse. One of the issues for men who might be hurt by their spouse or their spouse's family is that there is very little community support for them. There are no domestic-violence shelters for men. The police response can be homophobic and inadequate. In some cases, the police offer no protection at all to men who have been beaten up by their wives or in-laws. That can make it dangerous for a man who is in an abusive environment and is coming out.

The *Tyra* show did a segment on men who are abused by their wives and girlfriends. From the statistics they quoted, it appears that the phenomenon is not uncommon. Among the couples that Tyra interviewed were a big, muscular man and his girlfriend. He told her that he wouldn't marry her because of the abuse. He said, "Are you kidding? If we get married, it's just gonna get worse." He's right. It can get worse, as Drew's story below reveals. The marriage vow seems to give some people *carte blanche* to do what they want.

—Drew's Story—

Growing up, I had a horribly abusive family life. At the drop of a hat, my mother would pull out a belt, hanger, or anything else she could get her hands on to beat my siblings and me into submission. Many times I would lie in bed crying, alone, sore from being beaten, bleeding, bruised, feeling unloved, and wondering what in the world I'd done to deserve that kind of punishment.

Like most of the women in my life—my mother, my paternal grandmother, my various girlfriends—my wife was difficult. She was demanding and dramatic. When Susan didn't get her way, she'd create all kinds of chaos: screaming, hollering, crying, throwing things, and physically abusing me. She scratched me with her nails more times than I can count. People at work would ask me about the scratches on my neck and face, and I'd make excuses.

I remember having only one argument of any significance with Susan before we got married. It wasn't until that ring went on my finger that all hell broke loose.

Over time I began to realize there was nothing I could do to make this woman happy. But oddly it didn't occur to me to leave until years later. The till-death-do-us-part clause was hard-wired in my brain. I believed that when you make a vow, you take what you get and live with it. I never wanted to divorce. I always managed to put the blame for her anger on myself, and I somehow came to terms with the turmoil and drama in my life.

But then something happened that changed all that. I'd made an appointment to see my family doctor, and Susan scratched my neck the night before. The doctor asked me what the scratches were. I started to sob. At that moment, I was finally able to tell somebody what was going on in my life. She told me that I needed to get into therapy and make some changes in my life to stop the violence.

I'm a pretty muscular guy. Who would believe that a woman could kick my ass? Why didn't I hit her back? For one thing, I knew that if I hit her or physically harmed her in any way, I could have been thrown in jail. But that wasn't the only reason.

There were a few times I did hit her back, and I always regretted it. It's very difficult not to defend yourself when you're being attacked. So many times I just walked away. I was afraid that if I let myself go, I'd hurt her badly, and that's not what I wanted to do. That's not who I am. What was even worse than the fear of going to jail was my fear of descending to her level of drama and violence. Anytime you open up to fury and abuse like that, the outcome is never good.

It was all so ironic and transparent. The actions of my wife were the actions of my mother. The drama, the violence, and the chaos were all the same. It was all so familiar to me that I had no frame of reference that what was going on in my life was different from anyone else's. It was as though I had blinders on for thirty-six years—until that day my doctor called me out.

I didn't leave Susan until a few months later. The incident that led to my walking out started early one afternoon, when she called me at work. She had gotten into my computer and found that I'd been visiting gay websites. When she told me what she'd found, it was like a dream come true. I'd finally been outed! For a moment, I was euphoric, but then it hit me. I had to go home. I stayed at work as late as I could. I wanted to get myself together before I saw Susan.

When I got home, she was waiting for me in the kitchen. There was an odd calmness about her, but I could see in her eyes that a storm was brewing. She started to hurl accusations at me. I had been lying to her, hiding things from her, and cheating on her. I remember getting this weird smile on my face. I felt as if an enormous weight was lifting off my shoulders. She screamed that my head was so big I couldn't get it through our front doors. She also said that she thought my friend Tom and I were having an affair and that she'd called Tom's wife to tell her.

At that point, Susan hadn't touched me. Nothing physical had happened. I went into my home office and locked the door. I didn't want to be near her. She came to the door and asked me to let her in. I knew that tone in her voice. I thought that as long as I stayed in my office, I was safe.

When I wouldn't let her in, Susan kicked her foot through the six-panel solid-pine door. I turned around because the door was to my back, and I saw her face peeking through the hole she'd made. Her eyes had an insane glow in them. All I could think of was the iconic scene in *The Shining* in which Jack Nicholson peers smiling through a hole in a door that he's chopped with an ax in order to kill his wife and son. I cringed to myself and thought, *Here's Susieee.*

She broke into the room and tore into me. She threw me up against my desk, knocked me to the floor, and kicked and scratched and punched. It seemed to go on for hours. She was bruised too from me fighting back to defend myself from the worst physical abuse I'd ever gotten. Every time I tried to get out of the room, she'd knock me down. It amazes me how strong a human being can be in that kind of rage. I have no other memories of that night.

The next day I wasn't able to go to work. I knew that whether I was gay or straight, our marriage was over. And it was. I left.

I think Susan would have eventually killed me if I'd stayed. In an abusive relationship like ours, it takes two people to realize that there's a problem, and two people need to change it. When one person shifts as I did—*shift* is a term that my therapist used to describe what I did—the other person intensifies. Susan felt she was losing the control she'd had, and she didn't like it, so the violence just got worse. I left before the consequences were irreversible.

Abuse is something you should never tolerate. I learned that the hard way.

Since I left Susan, my life has been so much better for the obvious reason that I'm no longer being criticized and abused. When you're in that type of relationship, you're in the mindset of abuse, and you don't even know it. I'd get hit or berated and I wouldn't like it, but it never occurred to me that I could do anything about it. I was living life in a bubble. I thought there was something wrong with me. Susan has such a strong personality and was so controlling that I was always looking for how I could make things work. *What am I doing wrong? How can I change this?* What can I do better?

Leaving Susan allowed me to burst that bubble. I learned that, when you're in an abusive relationship, the only thing you can do to help yourself is to get away from the person who's abusing you. I was married to her and we had children so it was more complicated, but I had to get away.

In a way, having children gave me even more impetus to leave. I've learned that there's a cycle of abuse. A child who grows up in an abusive family is more likely to abuse others or to be abused as an adult. That was true for me, and I didn't want it to be my children's future. I was determined to break the cycle of abuse for them. To do that, I had to get away from Susan.

Since I left, my children don't know abusive behavior anymore, at least not from their parents. That's not what we do in our home.

—Staying Safe—

Drew lived through one sort of abuse, but there are environments in which coming out can be even more dangerous than his situation was. Just as there are cultures where women can get killed for dishonoring their families with their behavior (such as having an affair, getting raped, or being too provocative), there are also cultures where gay men and women put their lives at risk by coming out.

If that is the situation you are in, you need to protect yourself. Do whatever you need to do to be safe. That's number one. I also recommend that you get into therapy. There are counselors who can help you find the resources you need to get out of an abusive situation. Those services do exist. In addition, I can't imagine that anyone who's been abused or risked abuse by coming out would not benefit from therapy. Drew says that therapy has helped him live life as something other than a victim.

The recommendations I'm giving might be different depending on where you live. I'm writing this for an American audience. I don't know what it would be like to come out in India or Nigeria. What I'm recommending for Americans may not be feasible in another culture. The basic dilemma is the same—how to be true to yourself in a culture where it is shameful or sinful or wrong to be who you are. That dilemma is very different in different cultures. It's one thing to be shunned for coming out. It's a problem of a different magnitude to risk being killed for your sexual orientation.

If your life is at risk, you have a simple choice: pretend to be someone you're not or get the hell out of there. Sure, you can stay and fight for your right to be who you are, but do you really want to risk your life? Is being right worth your life?

—Safe Sex—

The other aspect of safety you need to consider in coming out is safe sex. Although this is an issue that all sexually active people need to deal with, it's something that's easy to neglect if you become sexually active after being married for years.

It's not unusual for a person leaving a straight marriage and coming out as gay to go through a period of acting like a fifteen year old—which for lack of a better word I would describe as *imprudent*. After spending years (perhaps a lifetime) being unsure of who you are, perhaps in a relationship in which you didn't quite fit, there can be a giddy freedom in coming out. Many people express that freedom by having lots of sex. It's not unusual for that giddiness to be accompanied by a lapse in better judgment, which is the hallmark in failing to practice safe sex. In the gay world, we call this period "gay adolescence."

I use the term here as though gays and lesbians own it, but I don't think that is accurate. I suspect that most people leaving a long-term relationship go through a similar phase regardless of their sexual orientation. I don't think there is much difference between gay adolescence and what most people (gay or straight) go through when they leave a long, exclusive relationship. In both cases, there is a period of discovery, where you no longer feel tethered to another person and you have a new freedom to express yourself.

That new freedom is sometimes an opening to risky behavior. As time goes on, maturity and common sense tend to return, and risky behavior tends to wane. Nevertheless, it is a good idea to be aware that gay adolescence exists. It is also a good idea, whether you are gay or straight, not to get involved in a serious relationship or make other major life decisions immediately after a serious breakup. (See Drew's interview for his account of going through gay adolescence.)

When I first came out, there was no way I wasn't using a condom. Now, if I'm in a relationship, using a condom may be optional, but I tend to err on the side of caution to protect myself. Because of the promiscuity in the gay community, however, the recommendation is for gay men to practice safe sex even with their partner, because partners can get infected. It's a crapshoot.

In the 1980s, when HIV and AIDS became epidemic and thousands of gay men died, the awareness of sexually transmitted diseases (STDs) grew in the gay community. But now, there is medication available that makes it possible to die of old age before you'd die of AIDS. In my view, the development of antiretrovirals has made many people in the gay community complacent about the risk of STDs and the practice of safe sex. I think that's particularly true among younger people. The fear of death is a powerful deterrent. Without it, there's sometimes apathy regarding safe sex.

My advice is to be smart about it and educate yourself about sexually transmitted diseases and how to keep yourself from being infected. It may be true that HIV/AIDS is no longer the death sentence it was in the past, but I've never met anyone with HIV or AIDS who wouldn't give anything to go back and undo the actions that resulted in him or her becoming infected.

In addition, HIV/AIDS is only one of many sexually transmitted diseases with which you can be infected. Some STDs are caused by bacteria, including gonorrhea (a drug-resistant strain of which is spreading around the globe), syphilis, Chlamydia, chancroid, and granuloma inguinale. Some are viral: HIV, HPV, CMV, herpes, some forms of hepatitis, and Molluscum contagiosum. Yeast infections, which are fungal, can also be sexually transmitted. The same is true of some parasite infections (crab lice and scabies) and the protozoal infection trichomoniasis.

There are a lot of good reasons to practice safe sex. Sexually transmitted disease is a burden on your immune system. It can make you more susceptible to other diseases. Even if you contract an STD that is not life threatening, it can be a burden on your time and resources, cutting down on your possibilities in life. The eighteenth-century British physician Thomas Fuller wrote, "Health is not valued till sickness comes." I suspect that many of the millions of people who are infected with sexually transmitted diseases would agree with the good doctor.

Rachel, a friend of mine, fell in love with and married a man who was infected with genital herpes. Before they became intimate, he told her that he had herpes, and for a long time they practiced safe sex. Once she was clear that they were going to spend the rest of their lives together, Rachel decided that they could stop using condoms. Ten years later, they divorced and she was single again. But now she had herpes, and as she started dating, she discovered there were lots of men who do not want an intimate relationship with a woman with an STD.

Unlike Rachel, who knew that she was exposing herself to genital herpes, most people are not aware that they are being infected when they contract an STD. They didn't think they could get infected from that person, or that way, or just that one time—or they just didn't think.

To protect yourself and others from sexually transmitted diseases, you need to think. You need to be aware of the risks of STDs and what you can do to keep yourself disease free. There are things you can do to protect yourself from STDs. The Resources section in the back of this book includes websites and organizations you can use to educate yourself about safe sex.

Knowing what to do isn't enough—you need to put into practice what you learn. To stay safe, you need to practice safe sex.

I think this is particularly true for men who are married to women and beginning to explore having sex with other men. I've known men who insist that they practice safe sex because they wear a condom when they have anal sex. They aren't aware that they can get an STD from oral sex. By not using protection during oral sex, they can contract gonorrhea or syphilis, and then take the disease they've picked up home to their wife.

That can happen in any relationship when one partner strays. In cases like that, the partner who's been cheated on has to deal with the emotional betrayal along with the fact that they've been given an STD. That's rough.

Whether you're gay or straight, I think it's important to act with integrity.

I believe that safe sex is a matter of responsibility and integrity. It's a matter of keeping yourself and those you love safe.

Chapter 11
Don't Underestimate How Difficult the Transition Can Be

"The truth will set you free, but first it'll piss you off."
—Kathy

One piece of advice that several of the people I interviewed gave was not to underestimate how difficult it can be to make the transition from the straight world to the gay world.

Drew was one of the men who spoke about this. "As good as things are for me now," he said, "I always tell people who are in a straight marriage and looking to come out not to underestimate how hard the transition can be."

When you come out as gay after being in a straight marriage, you go from being a member of the dominant culture to becoming part of a minority culture. Adam spoke about some of the aspects of life that change when you make that transition: "Being gay, there are lots of things I can't do now that heterosexuals can do. I can't walk down the streets of most cities and put my arm around a man and plant a big kiss on him. I could do that with a woman, but if I do it with another man there could be consequences. In some neighborhoods, I'd be nuts to do it. Could I go to a Steelers' game and do that? Hell, no. Could I go to a business convention and take a man with me to the dinner? No. It would be bad for business. I'm a very spiritual man. Could I really go to most churches in America and worship being who I am? No, I can't."

Adam said he thinks there are a lot of men who are open to having sexual experiences and sexual satisfaction with another man but who choose a traditional life because it's not as easy to be gay.

I can write about this only from my experience as a gay man. From what I understand from the women I've spoken with, it's very different for a woman to come out as a lesbian than it is for a man to come out as gay.

The world of gay men is a very, very physical world. Gay men are all about the physical. You'll run into a lot of attitude if you don't have the perfect build, or the perfect car, or the perfect house. Those are the kinds of things that matter. I'll be in a club talking with a little young thing who'll say to me, "Well, you're fat." Young gay men can be so rude. They can be ruthless. I'll answer back, "Didn't your mother feed you when you were growing up? Is that why you're so mean?" Other men commented on this aspect of gay life in their interviews. For example, Ben said, "It's important to know that you're never going to be free from judgment in the gay world."

It can be difficult to find intimacy with someone. In my experience, many gay men have a tough time being intimate. I'm not referring to sexual intimacy but to being intimate in sharing who they are. Of course I'm generalizing. There are many guys who are not like that. There are gay men who are in long-term committed relationships and share everything, just as married straight couples do. But most of the gay men I know are in and out of relationships like crazy. They just cannot, for whatever reason, find someone to settle down with.

Drew talked about this. He said, "There are friends of mine who've found really great relationships and partners. For some reason, I haven't yet. You may or may not find the relationship you're looking for because it might not be there. It hasn't been there for me—but then, it wasn't there for me in the straight world either."

I meet men who may not even be capable of maintaining a long-term relationship. Most people know that LTR stands for long-term relationship. In the gay world, it stands for long temporary relationship. My ex-partner is as old as I am and the longest relationship he's had was six years.

I know that a lot of straight women say the same thing: It's hard to find a good man who wants to settle down. I'm not sure what it is—maybe we're looking for something that doesn't exist.

Gay men and straight women have some things in common because we both partner with men. Whether the man you're dating is gay or straight, many men still have the same wiring in not being able to articulate their own thoughts and feelings and share them with you. When things get difficult, they'd rather just move on. They say, "I think I'll start over." "I need a fresh face." "I need somebody to make me feel younger." Good luck with that.

Drew explains this apparent shallowness as a lack of self-actualization. "One of the problems with gay men is that most are not anywhere near self-actualized—although that may be true of people in general," he said. "It may seem as though a person has his act together, but it's easy to be wrong."

He noted that he had an experience recently that exemplified that phenomenon. "I became reacquainted with someone I hadn't talked with in five years. He and I met in a chat room and, for the next two weeks, we talked by phone every day—sometimes for as long as three hours at a clip. It felt as though we were getting to know one another. It was great. One day, he stopped taking my calls for no reason. I don't know how you go from talking to someone for three hours a night and saying 'I like you' to all of a sudden nothing—where he's not even responding to my calls. I don't know if I said something to offend him or if he met someone else. I received no explanation whatsoever. I've had that happen countless times, and so have all my gay friends."

Drew said that in that situation, when the tables are turned—when he has been talking with somebody and realizes that the relationship is not going to work—he lets the other person know that it isn't working for him. "I try to be as cordial as possible," he explained. "I don't want to hurt anyone's feelings. But if it's not working for me, I've learned that it begins to hurt me more to continue down that path because I'm not being truthful with them and maybe not even with myself. It can be hard to be honest with people, but I find that telling the truth is so much more respectful than just disappearing."

Drew offered a possible explanation for what he sees as a relative lack of self-actualization among gay men. "I find that people who've been married and have kids have a sense that life is not just about us. We have a sense of being more than our own wants and needs. When someone like that comes out and meets people who have had nothing to commit themselves to except maybe their job or their dog, it can be a shock. Personally, I found it way harder to be a parent than I ever expected. Nothing in my life prepared me for the challenge it is. What I'm talking about is not unique to the gay world, but it has shown up as an issue for me in dating gay men."

It's my opinion and that of several of the men I interviewed that the later you come out in life, the more difficult the transition can be. As in any transition, you have to learn the ropes, and that can be harder when you're no longer young. A lot of men who divorce their wives and come out think, *Wow. I'm gay. This is going to be great.* Sometimes it's not. The French have a saying: The more things change, the more they stay the same. We make changes in order to have our lives be different, but many times those changes make no real difference at all. It's like changing the wallpaper in your dining room. It may look different, but it's not really.

Ben spoke about how it can be more difficult to find a new relationship as one gets older. "I think when you're younger," he said, "you have more hopes and you're more naïve. Somehow that allows you more grace earlier in life. As we get older, we become more set in our ways. I certainly am. It feels as if I've become wired to think *I don't need to deal with this bullshit.* Whenever I think that thought, I just want to go away and do my own thing. That doesn't make it easy to create a successful relationship."

As he was wrapping up his comments, Ben made an observation that I felt gave an important perspective to the topic of transitioning to being gay. "Coming out earlier doesn't make it easier today. It makes it easier next year, and five years from now, and fifteen years from now, because by then you'll have built a new life for yourself." I think Ben's perspective on this is significant given that, while he was married to Marin, he spent ten years going to gay bars trying to figure out if he wanted to live as a gay man.

I want to conclude this section with some words of advice and encouragement. First are some recommendations from Erin, whose number-one piece of advice is not to jump into another relationship too quickly. "I recommend you take your time," she counseled. "If you do leave your marriage, it's wise not to move into another relationship right away. Almost anyone who's been through a divorce knows that. That's true in heterosexual relationships and obviously it would be true in homosexual relationships also. My therapist advises people to wait four months for every year they've been married before getting into a new relationship. You have your own things to go through when you're the one who leaves."

Erin also gave advice about what to expect emotionally in making the transition from a straight marriage to coming out as gay. "Even when leaving your marriage is the right thing to do, know that you're still going to be sad. We think we should feel fine, and we don't feel fine. And along with feeling sad, we inevitably feel not sure at times that we're doing the right thing. I know women who've been divorced for ten years or more and still question if they made a mistake in leaving their husband. Their kids, if they hear their mother expressing that doubt, will usually say something like 'Are you crazy? You two were so incompatible.'"

I also want to offer some advice. One of the questions I asked when I looked at coming out was how do I meet people. Over time, I met people in two ways—in bars and through volunteerism. Without a doubt, I found the best way to meet people is by volunteering with organizations whose work you support.

I've recently started thinking about community as a series of concentric circles—a circle within a circle within a circle. The gay community can be seen that way. In the innermost circle are the movers and shakers who are at the heart of the community. These are the people you see at every event and fundraiser and party. They seem to know everyone, and everybody knows them. In the second circle are the people who come to events and parties, but participate less often or less intensely than people in the inner circle. The outer circle is the realm of people who are not interested in participating or simply don't know how to access the heart of the community. In the gay community, this is often where you'll find people who have recently come out. I have found that the easiest, most direct way to get to know people in a community—and to move closer to the heart of the community—is to volunteer.

There are plenty of groups you can volunteer with. You can meet good, strong people that way. I did. I still volunteer. In general, the same small group of people tends to volunteer. The good news about that is, if you do volunteer, you will tend to stand out as the new person. You'll meet lots of people, and they'll embrace the daylights out of you because you're a new face. It's a natural way to assimilate into the community and meet people you will want to get to know.

Final Thoughts

"If God had wanted me otherwise, He would have created me otherwise."
—Johann Wolfgang von Goethe

I believe that, gay or straight, it's up to each of us to create our life. There are things in life I have no control over such as the color of my skin, my height, and the family I was born into. There are also plenty of aspects of my life that I can do something about—my weight (I'm working on it), the color of my hair, what I do with my time, the people I share my life with, and what I envision and dream.

In the gay world, most things are gay-tainted. There's gay volleyball, gay softball, and gay bowling. There are gay bars and gay dance clubs. There are even gay neighborhoods in most sizeable cities. The straight world exists off somewhere else, and the two worlds don't mesh.

That's because historically homosexuals have been considered pariahs. Decent people didn't want homosexuals around unless they pretended to be like everyone else. Over time gays and lesbians who didn't want to pretend to be someone they're not started creating their own community.

The gay community is a phenomenal community. It's full of bright, creative people. Gay men design half the clothing you wear. Fran Lebowitz said, "If you removed all of the homosexuals and homosexual influence from what is generally regarded as American culture, you would pretty much be left with *Let's Make a Deal*." The gay community is segregated because gays segregate themselves.

I'm a gay man but I have children and I lived a straight life, so I live between both worlds. I exist in both worlds.

Last Sunday I was at my son's ice hockey banquet. To the other parents there, I'm just a normal father. I don't run around wearing a tiara or silver shoes. I don't go up to other parents and tell them I'm gay. I say, "Hi, I'm Mike." They either like me for who I am or they don't. I don't ask them what they do in their bedroom—I don't really care—and they don't ask me what I do in mine. I don't know if they know I'm gay. If they do, they don't treat me any differently. I exist in their world, and they exist in mine.

For a few days before the hockey banquet, my seventeen-year-old son didn't come home, and I didn't know where he was. I tried to track him down. I went to the homes of all his friends. Most of his friends were at the banquet on Sunday, and all their parents came up to me that night and expressed their concern about my son. They knew that I had been out looking for him. They were very helpful—texting me, talking to their kids about where they'd seen my son, and giving me suggestions about what to do next. I finally found him, and he was fine. I don't know what he was doing exactly, except that he was avoiding me.

Last weekend was an object lesson for me that I live in two worlds, and I'm the same person in both. I don't hide the fact that I'm gay, but I also don't lead with that aspect of who I am. I don't dress in brocade jackets in the gay world and baseball caps in the straight world. I have only one set of clothes. I don't ever become a flaming gay man. In fact, gay men often ask me if I'm straight. Others don't even come up to me because they think I'm straight or they're not sure. On the other hand, women sometimes approach me, especially once they find out I'm divorced and have children.

I'm just who I am. Being that way and being able to navigate in two normally separate worlds gives me a much bigger world to live in.

My point is that I create my life, just as we all do.

If you are in a straight marriage and questioning whether you are actually straight, it's easy to feel trapped by your circumstances. But you are not trapped. Having been in the situation you're in, I know how uncomfortable you probably feel. You have a choice to make, and I know from experience that there's no right choice and there's no wrong choice.

Writing this book is a dream come true for me. It has been an extremely emotional experience, bringing up so much of the pain and confusion I went through in coming out.

I learned a lot in that process, and I hope that reading this book has been as enlightening for you as writing it has been for me. Some of what I learned were things that I knew instinctively, but I became aware of them consciously as I read over my friends' stories. I learned that, while homosexuals are generally portrayed as stereotypes in our culture, none of the people who tell their stories in these pages fit the stereotypes of gay men or lesbian women.

All of us are average Americans. We all have (or are retired from) good jobs, and we all have families we love. None of us look or act gay or lesbian—whatever that might be. Many of the issues that we confronted in coming out are the issues that any person, regardless of sexual identity, confronts in divorce. *Am I making a mistake? Is this going to hurt my kids or my relationship with my kids? Maybe I should just forget it and not rock the boat.*

As I wrote this book, I became even more present to the many forms that homophobia takes. For example, at least five of the eight of us did not realize that we were homosexual until we were in our thirties. As Betty Hill explained to me early in the process of writing this book, we live in a culture in which people don't know themselves easily and we're all invited to conform to the majority. That's what most of us did. Unconsciously, we conformed to the majority culture and denied who we are until we couldn't deny it anymore.

Other examples of homophobia included the demeaning ways that loved ones responded to suspicions or admissions of our homosexuality: Trudy's mother telling her young daughter that she was going to hell; Kathy's fiancé giving her two weeks to "get fixed" after she told him that she was questioning her sexuality; and Grace's mother saying that she had to hide from her relatives the fact that Grace was with a woman.

Despite the difficulties that some of us experienced, all eight of us are happier and have more satisfying lives since coming out. That's not a recommendation that anyone should leave a marriage. I look at it more as a recommendation to tell the truth and live authentically. As I wrote at the beginning of this book, I do not advocate divorce. I advocate living with integrity, and I believe that telling the truth about who you are is an act of integrity that makes a difference for you and others.

That's not to say that it's easy to come out, especially if you're in a straight marriage. If you leave your marriage, things may get even tougher. According to the Holmes and Rahe Stress Scale, the only life event more stressful than divorce is the death of a spouse. In the case of people who leave a straight marriage to come out as gay, that stress is magnified immeasurably. They are dealing with the emotional trauma that anyone experiences going through the divorce process, while at the same time coming out.

All my friends whose stories are in this book had to muddle their way through this emotional minefield, generally with little support from family or friends. Most of us had to deal with this stress on our own. Those who did get support from friends and relatives found that, unless their loved ones were gay, they really didn't know how to help.

If you are in a straight marriage and not sure if you are straight or gay, I suggest that often the best course of action is to find a therapist or someone else you can talk with. The ideal is to find someone who can guide you through the process—regardless of what you ultimately choose to do.

Drew found a therapist whom he later discovered was a lesbian who had been in a straight marriage. He explained, "Before I knew she was a lesbian, Julie would give me advice that would just blow me away. I'd think, 'Gosh, she must talk to a lot of people like me!'" Drew came to find out later that Julie was able to give him such good advice because she had already gone through the process he was in.

As time goes on, there is more and more support available for people who are coming out and for the gay community in general. For someone coming out today, it is much easier to get the support you need.

I wrote this book to provide a resource for men and women who are homosexual (or questioning if they are) and in straight marriages. The stories I have compiled are the stories of my friends. We each wanted to share what we went through to show you that there is light at the end of the tunnel you're in. The way out of the darkness is to tell the truth—at least to yourself and ideally also to your spouse. There is power in being true to yourself and others. We hope that people who are not gay will also read our stories so that they can better understand what gays and lesbians go through when they try to make themselves adapt to the dominant (heterosexual) culture.

Most of us have come through very difficult times, and we have not only survived but also thrived in creating a new life. We all found ways to integrate ourselves into the gay and lesbian community. Most of us volunteer our time to support others in that community.

When I first came out, my partner and I would meet friends at a gay bar every week to watch *Will & Grace*. One particular night, as I described at the beginning of this book, there were five of us together at the bar. We had all been married to women, between us we had enough children to fill a small classroom, and we had all come out as gay. That night I wondered how many other people were out there who were in straight marriages and in fear of coming out the way we had.

I know many gay men who remain in straight marriages. They cheat on their wives with men and think nothing of it. I try to talk to them about the dangers of what they're doing. Most of the men I talk to don't seem to care. I have to believe their wives know and simply choose to ignore that their husbands are leading a double life. Maybe I'm naïve to believe that or unwilling to accept the cruelty of the alternative.

If there is one thing to take away from this book, it is that you can be true to yourself. You can live authentically. If you do come out, you may struggle to be happy, and you will probably question your choices over and over again. As time goes on, any wounds that were created by coming out will heal. The more people you come out to, the more you will garner their support and love.

At times I still have trouble coming out to people, but every time I do, I am stronger for it. I can feel the energy change with the person I'm talking to and they almost always become supportive. A bond is created that did not exist before. Recently I came out to some friends that I grew up with. Afterward they said some kind, supportive things to me.

For me, coming out is the thing to do to be myself. It's freedom. It's lifting a weight that has sat on my shoulders for most of my life. My experience is that other people want me to be happy. Most people are fair. Most people realize that the LGBT community has been put down long enough, and it's time to be on the right side of history.

My love goes out to you all. Be true to yourself, be strong, and be loved the way you need to be loved. It's your time.

Acknowledgments

It's been an honor and a joy to work with the many people who have been my partners in creating this book. I want to thank my family and friends for their encouragement and support.

In particular, I want to express my gratitude to my seven friends whose stories are included in these pages. This project has not been easy for any of us. Telling your story often dredges up memories and emotions you'd probably rather forget. Each of us has gone through some emotional discomfort in recounting our stories for publication. Thank you all for your willingness to share your stories and to allow your successes and your mistakes be an inspiration to others.

I also want to offer my thanks to those who have helped make this book a reality, including:

Betty Hill, who generously shared with me her knowledge of the LGBT community and the issues people in straight marriages deal with in coming out.

Anne Fleming, who connected me with Deborah Gouge.

Deborah Gouge, who has worked with me closely as my editor to make this book come to life.

Camden Leeds, who created a cover design and layout that is spot on for the look I wanted this book to have.

Notes

1 "Data from Alfred Kinsey's Studies," The Kinsey Institute for Research in Sex, Gender, and Reproduction, http://www.kinseyinstitute.org/research/ak-data.html#homosexuality (accessed January 2, 2014).

2 "Data from Alfred Kinsey's Studies," The Kinsey Institute for Research in Sex, Gender, and Reproduction.

3 Alfred C. Kinsey, Wardell B. Pomeroy, and Clyde E. Martin, *Sexual Behavior in the Human Male* (Philadelphia: W. B. Saunders Co., 1948), p. 639.

4 Benedict Carey, "Straight, Gay, or Lying? Bisexuality Revisited," *The New York Times*, July 5, 2005. www.nytimes.com/2005/07/05/health/05sex.html?pagewanted=all (accessed January 6, 2014).

5 Gerulf Rieger, Meredith L. Chivers, and J. Michael Bailey, "Sexual Arousal Patterns of Bisexual Men," *Psychological Science* 16, no. 8 (2005): 579–584.

6 Benedict Carey, "Straight, Gay, or Lying? Bisexuality Revisited."

7 David Badash, "Study Shows How Many Americans Are Gay, Lesbian, Bisexual, Transgender," *The New Civil Rights Movement*, April 7, 2011. http://thenewcivilrights movement.com/study-shows-how-many-americans-are-gay-lesbian-bisexual-transgender/news/2011/04/07/18551 (accessed January 3, 2014).

8 Jane Gross, "When the Beard Is Too Painful to Remove," *The New York Times*, August 3, 2006. http://www.nytimes.com/2006/08/03/fashion/03marriage_bg.html?_r=5&ex=1154836800&en=c18780d5fa634c82&ei=5087 (accessed January 3, 2014).

9 Jane Gross, "When the Beard Is Too Painful to Remove."

10 Preeti Pathela and others, "Can Doctors Use Self-Reported Sexual Identity as a Reliable Indicator of Sexual Behavior?" *Annals of Internal Medicine* 145, no. 6 (September 19, 2006): 1–57. http://annals.org/article.aspx?articleid= 728861 &result Click=3 (accessed January 6, 2014). This article is a summary of the full report below.

11 Preeti Pathela and others, "Discordance Between Sexual Behavior and Self-Reported Sexual Identity: A Population-Based Survey of New York City Men," *Annals of Internal Medicine* 145, no.6 (September 19, 2006): 416-425. http://annals.org/article.aspx? articleid=728543&resultClick=3#Results (accessed January 6, 2014).

Resources

The Body

A website that is the complete HIV/AIDS resource. It includes articles about and links to HIV/AIDS hotlines and organizations.
www.thebody.com

CenterLink

With a directory listing 200 community centers, CenterLink is a resource you can use to find an LGBT community center.
www.lgbtcenters.org

Centers for Disease Control and Prevention

The federal government's Centers for Disease Control and Prevention provides a wide range of health information on its website. Here are some of the topics that may be relevant to you:

> Information about sexually transmitted diseases, including treatment recommendations
> www.cdc.gov/std/default.htm

> How to prevent sexually transmitted diseases
> www.cdc.gov/std/prevention/default.htm

> Information about HIV/AIDS, syphilis, and viral hepatitis for men who have sex with men
> www.cdc.gov/hiv/risk/gender/msm/

> Information about HIV among women
> www.cdc.gov/hiv/risk/gender/women/index.html

> LGBT health topics and resources
> www.cdc.gov/lgbthealth/

Information about LGBT health services, including hotlines, social networks, and health clinics
www.cdc.gov/lgbthealth/health-services.htm

Information about gay and bisexual men's health
www.cdc.gov/msmhealth/

Information about health topics and resources for lesbians and bisexual women
www.cdc.gov/lgbthealth/women.htm

Equality Federation

Since 1997, the Equality Federation has worked throughout the U.S. to build leadership, strengthen state-based LGBT organizations, and make progress on critical LGBT issues.
http://equalityfederation.org

Freedom to Marry

Launched in 2003, Freedom to Marry is the campaign to win the right to marry for same-sex couples nationwide.
www.freedomtomarry.org

Gay, Lesbian & Straight Education Network

Begun in 1990 as a small group of dedicated teachers in Massachusetts, GLSEN is now the leading national education organization focused on ensuring safe schools for all students.
www.glsen.org

GLAAD

Begun in 1985, GLAAD is the nation's LGBT media-advocacy organization, promoting understanding, increasing acceptance, and advancing equality.
www.glaad.org

Human Rights Campaign

Founded in 1980, the Human Rights Campaign is the largest civil rights organization working for equal rights for lesbian, gay, bisexual, and transgender Americans.

www.hrc.org

The It Gets Better Project

The It Gets Better Project started with a YouTube video created in September 2010 by author Dan Savage and his partner Terry Miller. They posted the video to give hope to LGBT youth who are being bullied. That first video—with its message to young people that it does get better—has inspired more than 50,000 user-created videos that have been viewed more than 50 million times.

www.itgetsbetter.org

Lambda Legal

Founded in 1973, Lambda Legal is the oldest and largest national legal organization whose mission is to achieve full recognition of the civil rights of lesbians, gay men, bisexuals, transgender people, and those with HIV through impact litigation, education, and public policy work.

www.lambdalegal.org

Married Gay

This is a website started in 1999 for men and women who are gay, lesbian, or bisexual and their opposite-sex spouses or partners.

www.marriedgay.org

The National Center for Lesbian Rights (NCLR)

NCLR has been advancing the civil and human rights of lesbian, gay, bisexual, and transgender people and their families through litigation, legislation, policy, and public education since it was founded in 1977.

www.nclrights.org

The National Gay and Lesbian Task Force

Since the late 1970s, the National Gay and Lesbian Task Force has been working to build the grassroots power of the LGBT community to achieve equality. Its work includes training activists, supporting state and local organizations to organize legislative campaigns, and through its Policy Institute providing research and policy analysis to support equality.
www.thetaskforce.org

National Resource Center on LGBT Aging

Established in 2010, the National Resource Center on LGBT Aging is the only technical assistance resource center in the U.S. intended to improve services and support to LGBT older adults.
www.lgbtagingcenter.org

The Next Family

This website is a diverse community where modern families meet—including urbanite families, adoptive families, in vitro parents, interracial families, same sex parents, and single parents.
http://thenextfamily.com

Persad Center

Founded in 1972, Persad is a human service organization serving the LGBTQ (lesbian, gay, bisexual, transgender, queer and questioning) communities and the HIV/AIDS communities across western Pennsylvania. Although it is not a national or international service provider as the other organizations listed here are, I wanted to include Persad in this list because in Chapter 2 I wrote about it and its director Betty Hill.
https://persadcenter.org

PFLAG

Founded in 1972, PFLAG is the nation's largest family and ally organization for LGBT people. PFLAG has over 350 chapters and 200,000 members and supporters, including parents, families, friends, and straight allies of people who are lesbian, gay, bisexual, and transgender.
www.pflag.org

Prime Timers

A social organization that provides older gay and bisexual men the opportunity to enrich their lives, Prime Timers was started in 1987 and now has more than 80 chapters throughout North America, Europe, and Australia.
www.primetimersww.com

SAGE

Founded in 1978 in New York City, SAGE (Services & Advocacy for GLBT Elders) is the largest and oldest organization in the United States dedicated to improving the lives of lesbian, gay, bisexual, and transgender older adults. SAGE's mission is to take the lead in addressing issues of aging in the LGBT community.
www.sageusa.org

TED Talks

I am including two TED Talks by Brené Brown as resources because I believe they can be of value to anyone who is coming out. The first is The Power of Vulnerability. The second is Listening to Shame. They were filmed in June 2010 and March 2012 respectively. Brown is a research professor at the University of Houston Graduate College of Social Work.
www.ted.com/talks/brene_brown_on_vulnerability
www.ted.com/talks/brene_brown_listening_to_shame

The Trevor Project

Founded in 1998, The Trevor Project is the leading national organization providing crisis intervention and suicide prevention services to lesbian, gay, bisexual, transgender, and questioning (LGBTQ) young people.
www.thetrevorproject.org

About the Author

Michael Testa is a business owner and twenty-nine-year veteran of the information-technology industry. His company was named by the *Pittsburgh Business Times* as one of the top 25 information-technology consulting firms in the city. In 2007, Pittsburgh's mayor nominated Mike's business for the ICIC Inner City 100, a prestigious list of the fastest-growing companies in America's inner cities.

Mike is the vice president of Equality Pennsylvania, and a certified member of the National Gay and Lesbian Chamber of Commerce (NGLCC). He is also the founder and chairman of the Gay and Lesbian Executive Committee, a professional networking organization in Pittsburgh that is becoming part of the NGLCC.

Mike came out in his mid-thirties while he was still married. Now divorced, he lives outside Pittsburgh, Pennsylvania with his two sons.

When Opposites No Longer Attract is his first book.

Mike can be reached through his website, **www.testapublishing.com.**

30452920R00076